What people are saying about

Life...Don't Miss It

"This book shimmers with a rare blend of life experiences that will change your life. It is easy to see why Gary is a highly sought after and accomplished speaker on this subject, pure genius!"

—Jim Dowd

1995 Stanley Cup Champion, NJ Devils

"I procrastinated starting to read the book...I was too busy...I then couldn't put it down....kind of like life, eh? *Life...Don't Miss It*...seize the moment!"

—David Booth

*Former President, Global Sales and Marketing
Computer Sciences Corporation*

"A must read...Gary provides absolute clarity on how
to get the most out of your life...and he's doing it!"

—Roger Dow
President & CEO
U.S. Travel Association

"Our hectic, fast paced schedules and demanding careers have
a tendency to become the focus and priority in our lives and
result in us losing perspective of work-life balance. To achieve
full contentment, we need to continuously level set and be
reminded of what is truly important in life. I found that this
story teller like message, based on Gary's life experiences,
really resonates and reminds me to keep the right things
in perspective—to strive and achieve my full life worth."

Grover Smith
VP Global Accounts, Cisco Systems, Inc.

"Gary's unique insights on personal development
have been very beneficial to our company for many
years—reading this book will show you why!"

—David Marriott
Chief Operating Officer
America's Eastern Region
Marriott

"Business and life can swallow you whole. I have seen it happen. Great people lose their way and become caught up in things that ultimately don't matter—the result of which can be dramatically reduced professional effectiveness and a potentially disrupted personal life. The first time I met Gary, I knew he had it all figured out...He really gets it."

–Lawrence Calcano
Chairman & CEO, Bite Tech, Inc.

"As the first woman to have climbed Mount Everest twice, I understand the importance of finding your calling and living life to the fullest. Gary's story is authentic and honest, as he shares his journey to finding what truly matters in life. His insights and lessons are invaluable."

–Cathy O'Dowd
Speaker, author, adventurer

"*Life… Don't Miss It* is one of the most important books you could ever read at any age! In listening to CEOs give sage advice to students over the last 30 years, I have come to appreciate when someone has hand-carved a powerful, compelling summary of the 'right' advice."

–Roger Jenkins
Professor and Dean
Farmer School of Business, Miami University

Life...
Don't Miss It.
I *Almost* Did.

Life...
Don't Miss It.
I *Almost* Did.

How I Learned to
Live Life to Its Fullest

Gary Kunath

Advantage®

Published by Advantage, Charleston, South Carolina.
Member of Advantage Media Group.

ADVANTAGE is a registered trademark and the Advantage colophon is a trademark of Advantage Media Group, Inc.

Printed in the United States of America.

ISBN: 978-159932-269-8
LCCN: 2011905666

This publication is designed to provide accurate and authoritative information in regard to the subject matter covered. It is sold with the understanding that the publisher is not engaged in rendering legal, accounting, or other professional services. If legal advice or other expert assistance is required, the services of a competent professional person should be sought.

Advantage Media Group is proud to be a part of the Tree Neutral® program. Tree Neutral offsets the number of trees consumed in the production and printing of this book by taking proactive steps such as planting trees in direct proportion to the number of trees used to print books. To learn more about Tree Neutral, please visit www.treeneutral.com. To learn more about Advantage's commitment to being a responsible steward of the environment, please visit www.advantagefamily.com/green

Advantage Media Group is a leading publisher of business, motivation, and self-help authors. Do you have a manuscript or book idea that you would like to have considered for publication? Please visit www.amgbook.com or call 1.866.775.1696

To my parents, Frank and Fern Kunath.

I love you and miss you.

This is for you.

Acknowledgments

I have many people to thank for many things. In regards to this book being completed, I owe a great deal of thanks to Laura Gullotti, who has stood beside me unwaveringly and gave me motivation and encouragement to make this project happen. She has always been there for me. My life is better because of her.

To Mike Veeck, a dear friend who has added to my life in ways he will never know. I am honored that you found it worth your while to be my friend and the next time I get the wild idea that I can stay up until morning, smoking cigars and drinking great scotch with you, please put me to bed early before I hurt myself again.

To all of those people that took the time to read the book in its rough-draft form and provide endorsements for it: David Marriott, Lawrence Calcano, Roger Dow, Cathy O'Dowd, Jim Dowd, Grover

Smith, Dave Booth, and Roger Jenkins, I cannot thank you enough. I have tremendous respect for each of you and I am proud that you would agree to be a part of this project. It means a great deal to me.

To my good friend Peter Benedetto, who has always supported me, and most of all, has been a close friend to me through thick and thin. Thank you for being you.

To my sister, Chris Hanna, I will never forget how good you were to Mom and Dad, especially in their last days. You have a permanent place in my heart.

To my three sons, Dan, Dave and Tom Kunath, you will never know how much each of you mean to me.

To my good friend Mark Salsbury, you have always been the kind of friend who inspires me, makes me feel good to be around and whom I can always count on. You are a true 1 percenter. One more thing, I will always be better looking than you.

To all my lifelong neighborhood friends, Doug and Larry Riedman, George Aylesworth, Bryan "Booney" Acee, Bobby Jackson, Rich Albigese and Lynn Dembrow, I am proud that we always have been and always will be friends.

To all the great people at Advantage Publishing, I could not have done it without you. To Adam Witty, I am very proud of the man you have become.

Thank you to all those who have shared with me ideas, concepts or conversations over the years that have made it into this book in some fashion or other: Neil Kimball, Dan Migala, Tom Morris, Midnight Mike, Bob Burnap, Ron Weaver, Russell Simmons, and Rocket Ismail.

Foreword
by Mike Veeck

I know Gary Kunath. He is a friend of mine. I know him where he lives. So will you, when you read *Life…Don't Miss It (I Almost Did) How I Learned to Live Life to Its Fullest*. Kunath is a lecturer. A speaker in the popular jargon, but to me that is like referring to Demosthenes as a street corner pastor.

I have watched him take 57 minutes and transform an audience into a band of brothers…a group of believers. A mob dedicated to a peaceful revolution in the work place.

In a mix of student athlete (which he was) and a dose of improvisational comedian (which he was not), Kunath creates a business model that allows the human condition to contribute their very best to achieve optimum corporate performance. They are not mutually exclusive.

The first time I heard his Value Creation Theory, I heard the revolution of angry, marching employees strangled by overfed, bloated corporate structures governing by fear.

We have only to fear ourselves. Early in his career, as he watched thousands of jobs being terminated, he struggled to make sense of the old order. Unable to make sense of it, he created a new order. He focused on the only thing that was totally in his control, his life and the joy and contentment surrounding it.

Scar tissue can be a beautiful thing. This life/work balance for which Kunath advocates is not easily won. It does not come by way of the motivational dilettantes who litter the workplace. It is battle tested, scored, sometimes painful but always optimistic.

His chapter on Last Lecture to Your Family, where he shares a letter he wrote to his son, has a haunting refrain of STOP – SAVOR – ENJOY. He makes us believe that balance is possible, not some unreachable goal available only to theorists. But you want to know something, this letter was real; I read it when it was only a private epistle. I loved it then (as a matter of fact I stole the idea) and you'll love it now.

Kunath is a very funny man. Funny men are everywhere. He has a voice that will make you laugh. Then, wake you up in the middle of the night wondering if it was really funny. Go ahead, turn the page. My guess is he'll keep you up all night.

Table of Contents

CHAPTER ONE

Life Worth
or
Net Worth?

"The problem with being in the rat race is that
even if you win the race, you're still a rat."

–Lily Tomlin

"It is much more important to be significant than it is to
be successful…the difference is that significance is all about
helping others succeed, success is about helping yourself."

–Raghid "Rocket" Ismail

M any people focus on the wrong things in life until something whacks them on the side of their head and forces them to think about what they truly value and to assess just how far away they are from achieving happiness and "life worth." What I mean by "life worth" is the joy and contentment you get from life. Pretty simple if you ask me. Pretty simple if you ask anybody, really. What I've learned from my experiences is that the things I thought truly were the essence of happiness and life worth had absolutely *nothing* to do with either.

The Difference Between Life Worth and Net Worth

What I know for sure is that money doesn't make you rich. Money is one of the things I thought for sure would give me life worth and prove to be the key to lasting happiness. So I worked hard for it. It consumed me for a short period in my life. What I now know is that nothing could be further from the truth. Studies prove that people with money are, as a whole, less happy than people without money. The reason is that once you have money, then the myth of how your life will be better with money is erased. If you are mean without money, you will be mean with money. If you treat people poorly without money, you will act the same when you have it. Money changes nothing about you; it just allows you to buy more things. However, money also attracts more freeloaders who want handouts, more people with investments that can't miss, more relatives whom you have never seen before or have never called you, but now need a loan and more so-called friends and relatives who keep their hands deep in their pockets when the dinner bill arrives. Most people who have won the lottery claim they are worse off after winning than before.

I have been on both sides of the wealth divide. I remember having to take money out of my son's piggy bank just to be able to buy pizza for the family on a Friday night. Back then I thought, "Boy, if I won the lottery things would be different. If I was a CEO making tons of cash, all my worries would go away. I could have cool cars, a big house, designer clothes and my life would be perfect. If I was only rich." At that time, I thought that net worth automatically gave you life worth. It's pretty easy to think that way when you have no money or have low net worth. The truth is that I know a lot of people with high net worth whom I consider miserable failures as human beings. These are not stupid people. They were smart enough to achieve a high net worth, so you have to give them credit for that. The real question is, at what cost did they gain net worth? What part of their lives did they sacrifice for it? And more importantly, can they salvage their lives? Is there still time or is it too late?

I will never forget the farewell speech of the CEO of a Fortune 500 company whose retirement party I attended. After he took the microphone, this impressive and accomplished executive told the crowd of about 400 people that he knew many in the room wanted to know what it takes to do his job, to be the CEO. And he was going to tell them exactly what it takes. I watched as all the young anointed ones, the fast-trackers and future executive stallions, took out their pens and prepared to receive the career launch code to the top. Then the CEO told them that three weeks ago he was walking his daughter down the aisle at her wedding. As he was walking her down the aisle, on this most important day in their lives, he realized that he didn't know what his daughter's favorite color was. He could not tell you the title of her favorite book, or any book she had ever read for that matter. He couldn't even tell you what the last name of her best friend was. "That's what it takes to do this job," he concluded. "And if you want the job, you can have it."

In that one moment, I saw a man who had tremendous net worth but no life worth. This poor soul was a captain of industry, but not even a deckhand in his own life. He had missed so many of the most important moments of his life and he knew it. The sadness in his voice was mixed with bitterness and resentment of his job. But mostly he was angry with himself for the time he missed with his daughter and the rest of his family. He knew he could never get back that time and those memories he never got to make. What hurt the most was the recognition that buying his family nice things and sending his children to nice schools was no substitute for the one thing his family truly needed all those years: him. It didn't have to be that way. He now understood that the only reason you should care about your net worth is to underwrite your life worth. He learned the hard way that money doesn't make you rich.

Avoid the Net Worth Trap

The big question everyone must answer is, what is going to drive you and what are your priorities? In other words, will you focus on achieving net worth or life worth? When asked this question directly, everyone answers, "Life worth, of course." But in reality that is seldom how it works. If you focus on acquiring net worth and you are successful, it is a very intoxicating spin cycle that can easily take you in and not spit you out. Let me say up front that I completely understand focusing on acquiring net worth if you cannot afford the basics that people need just to live. You need to acquire things like food, shelter and clothing, and if you don't have those things, your first priority should be getting them. The real question is, what do you do after those needs are met? It is okay to focus on net worth as long as you know it is simply a vehicle to achieving life worth, but you must be able and willing to know when enough is enough. Also, you should refrain from competing with others. Envy is a waste of time because you already have everything you need. No matter how rich you become there will always be someone with more than you. Heck, there are people who make Bill Gates look like a middle-class guy.

In 1983, I began working for AT&T and spent the next 14 years in sales and sales training. In the early stages of my employment, I was focused on being a good corporate soldier and I believed in the system that if you performed, you would be rewarded. The rewards were more money, promotions, titles, prestige, and visibility with peers and with top executives in the hopes that maybe one day you could be a top executive too. So I worked hard: long weekends, conference calls on Fridays at 5 p.m., and leaving for business trips early on Sunday and returning home late Friday only to do it all over the next week. I was not alone by any means. I saw many people who believed the same thing and did exactly what I did for the company. They shaped their family lives around what the company's needs were. They even placed their families second and moved to any location the company required because they believed the company would take care of them in the end and do the right thing for them. AT&T was headquartered in New Jersey, and people wrangled to get to HQ because that was where the action was and where all the heavy breathers resided. To really ascend up the corporate ladder at AT&T, you had to move to New Jersey. If you wanted a career path with real potential then you *had* to do a tour of duty at HQ in New Jersey. It's funny because we actually did call it "a tour of duty," like it was joining the military and serving overseas in a theater of war. Rotate in for a couple of years and then rotate out with a nice promotion. That was the promise. If you were a high flyer and ambitious, you thought, "Sounds good to me, let's roll. My family will understand being uprooted and placing our future in the hands of AT&T and its management team. After all, they care about me." Plus, the transfer was only for two years, and AT&T promised to give you a letter saying that the company would transfer you back to the field in two years, they just couldn't guarantee where.

What I learned from others who were seduced to HQ was that this letter was not worth the paper it was printed on and that working at HQ with all the other high flyers was like swimming in a shark tank. You had to deal with people undercutting you, politics and favoritism, and the kiss-ups were at a whole new level. AT&T headquarters was the big leagues. Guys would bring two suit jackets to work with them, one to hang on their office wall after 5 p.m. (and leave their office lights still on) to give the appearance that they were working another 12-14 hour day in case a boss happened to walk by, and the other jacket to wear home as they snuck out the back door. Working at HQ was like putting a bunch of scorpions in a bottle. Even if you did not want to play the game, someone still kicked you just to make sure you were dead and not a threat to them or their career plans. Plus, New Jersey was an expensive place to live and most promotions from the field to HQ were accompanied by a modest $5,000-$7,000 annual raise, which was not enough to buy one Happy Meal a month at McDonald's after taxes.

Then a funny thing happened: AT&T went from being a monopoly to having to compete in the free market. That meant they had to streamline the business and their employee base. Now I don't blame AT&T a bit for doing what they had to do to become competitive. That's how business needs to function. AT&T did it legally and for the most part as fairly as they could. Still that doesn't change the fact that you are now out of work. As a young man in my early 20s, what happened at AT&T showed me very clearly that maybe I wasn't the most important thing to the company. Maybe *the company* was the most important thing to the company. I saw thousands of people lose their jobs. People who had given their lives to AT&T were now out of work and whatever hardships they put their families through from traveling, working long hours and getting transferred numerous times to new locations where they knew no one and had to start over with new schools, new doctors, new neighbors, and being farther from their homes, was all for nothing. All the collateral damage to their families they created by being a good corporate soldier, going everywhere they were asked and doing what they were told to cash in on the elusive pot of gold at the end of the rainbow was for a pot of gold that never came. It had proved to be a poor investment of their time and of themselves. Those people who had placed their families and personal lives on the rear burner to acquire net worth, got caught up in that spin cycle and truly missed the opportunity to build life worth. Many sacrificed life worth for many years. Fortunately I never went to HQ, as watching all this made me realize that I wanted no part of that. The cost was way too high.

I was fortunate in that I was able to keep my job. Clearly though, the rules were different. The corporate climate changed forever, as did my outlook. Even though I kept my job, I felt a lot like the turkey still in the pen the day after Thanksgiving. I felt relieved, but I knew Christmas was coming.

Make Yourself Employable Because Nobody Is Essential

I learned two very significant things from this experience. The first was that I would never let myself be in a position where a corporation would decide my future or would dictate whether I stay or go. After what I saw at AT&T, I would call the shots on whether or not I stayed or went. From that point forward my main goal was not to be an employee, but to be EMPLOYABLE. That meant I needed to increase my marketability and value so I could control my future.

To make myself employable, I took advantage of and leveraged all the corporate resources and experiences available so I could build my overall marketability and do it on my terms. This did not mean being a bad employee, just a very smart, purposeful employee. I created more options for myself that allowed me to work in any environment, particularly those that would be good for me personally and professionally. I don't just want to be happy with my work life or my home life—I want to be happy with my WHOLE life. That is the goal. Today, I counsel people everywhere I go that they need to be employable and independent of the company they work for so that they are the ones who decide their future, not the organization. If your work environment does not add to your life worth, ultimately you need to go somewhere that does or create your own environment, as I did later in my life.

The second thing I learned from AT&T is no matter who you are or how important you may think you are to an organization, you're not. I know people who are so consumed with their jobs that they work when they are sick, defer or never take vacations, and work while at home or on weekends when they have days off because they think the company needs them. They are nuts. The truth is that you are a shark tooth. Don't ever forget that. Sharks have many rows of teeth and when one tooth falls out, the tooth behind it simply pops into its place and replaces it. The shark doesn't even know it lost a tooth. I hate to say it, but that's what people are to an organization. When you leave, someone simply pops up in your place and soon no one even knows you are gone. Giving your life to the company and not to your family is crazy. *Never, ever* put your job or work before family.

Spend Most of Your Time on What Matters Most

Don't get me wrong. I fully understand that there are times when you have to do things for your job that affect your personal life. I get that. But be conscious of the limits you place on those things and put yourself in a highly marketable position to make a move if the company continuously interferes with your life worth. I have seen so many people at their jobs trying to be a hero to strangers when they really need to be a hero to the people who will be crying at their funerals. They are the only ones who matter.

The quest for net worth at the cost of life worth is not a good trade-off. A truly rich person is not the one who has the most, but the one who needs the least. The only reason to focus on net worth is to underwrite life worth. I promise you that in the end no one will care what kind of car you drove when you were 35 or the square footage of the largest home you ever owned. What will count and what does matter is what people remember about you. What kind of son or daughter were you? What kind of brother or sister were you? What will your children say about how great a mother or father you were to them? How great a friend were you? Did you make a difference in someone's life? Is the world just a little better because you roamed the planet? That is the stuff that matters.

That is where you spend your time. That is life worth. I know plenty of people who have big bank accounts but can count on one hand the number of their children's birthdays they actually have been home to enjoy, just like that CEO who hardly knew his own daughter. On the other side, I know people who are barely breaking even that are some of the happiest people and I consider many of them the most successful people I know. They enjoy life and all the great things that come with it. Every day and every minute.

The Egyptians believe that when you die you are asked two questions about your life. Your answers dictate where you will spend eternity. The two questions are:

Did you find joy in this life?

Did your life bring joy to others?

When you think of your life in those simple terms and can answer "yes" to both questions then you did pretty good.

The best definition of success I ever heard was from an entrepreneur who defined it as, "Applause at home." You can't say it any better than that.

"We've learned how to make a living, but not a life. We've added years to life but not life to years. We've been all the way to the moon and back but have trouble crossing the street to meet a new neighbor. We've conquered outer space but not inner space. These are the times of big men but small character, of steep paychecks and shallow relationships, of two incomes and more divorce, of fancier houses but more broken homes."

–George Carlin

CHAPTER TWO

The Gift of Adversity and the Need to Believe in Something Bigger Than You

"I would much rather act as though there is a God and be right than act as though there isn't and be wrong."

—C.S. Lewis

"The price of anything is the amount of life you exchange for it."

—Henry David Thoreau

Bad things happen to good people. Life is much bigger than any individual and it will deal you things that will bring you to your knees. Everyone gets their turn in the barrel. Adversity plays no favorites; it finds us all one way or another. Some of us experience adversity early in our lives, some of us later in our lives. Some of us get it all at once in multiples and some of us experience it over time. Make no mistake; adversity is an immutable fact of life. In the movie *Unforgiven,* the sidekick of Clint Eastwood's ruthless gunslinger and killer has just shot and killed someone for the first time and he tries to justify it by saying, " Well, I guess he had it coming." Eastwood responds, "We all got it coming, kid."

You really cannot talk about living if you don't talk about the tests we face throughout our lives. The death of a loved one, sickness, loss of a job or home, divorce, substance abuse, addiction, financial ruin, being the victim of a crime or having physical or mental challenges are some of the things we may face over the course of our lives. These are difficult things to talk about, but you need to know that if you do not believe in something bigger than you, these things will crush you. They are much bigger than any one person and it is impossible to stand all alone when these adversities pay you a visit.

I am speaking from experience on this one. I got divorced and lost everything I owned. I had an alcoholic family member who attempted suicide and I had 30 seconds on the telephone to convince him to put down the gun and not shoot himself. I watched both of my parents pass away; one from cancer and the other from a pancreatic aneurism. All of this happened in just two years. Pretty tough stuff, but everyone faces tough stuff.

Distinguish or Extinguish?

Believe it or not, I am convinced that we all truly *need* adversity in our lives because it is the only way you can discover who you truly are. Anyone can be a rock star when times are perfect, but adversity brings out who you are at your core. Adversity can either extinguish you or distinguish you. It's your call, and it totally depends on how you choose to respond. I once had a business associate who used a mountain-climbing analogy to describe how people react to adversity. He said you can be a quitter, a camper or a climber. Quitters simply give up when adversity strikes. Campers stop and hole up, do nothing and wait to see what happens. Climbers keep going and get stronger as they go. For some reason I have always been a climber. Adversity has always made me stronger.

I was very close to both of my parents. We had a great relationship. There was never a day that went by that we didn't talk and they always supported me and were proud of me, even when they had no reason to be. Those were the kind of parents I had, and I knew I was very lucky. My dad and mom were inseparable. Even in his 80s, the first thing my father would do when he woke up was to make my mom her coffee and bring it to her in her favorite chair with a small towel to place on her lap in case it spilled. They walked everywhere together holding hands.

It just never dawned on me that there would ever be a day when I wouldn't have them. It sounds goofy, but my parents both looked and acted many years younger than they were and my dad could still out-walk me any day of the week. Both of them were very funny people and they loved to laugh.

My dad was a navigator/bombardier in the U.S. Air Force and flew 45 missions over Germany in World War II. He won the Distinguished Flying Cross for bravery. That is one of the highest Medals of Honor one can receive for bravery, and the funny thing is that he never mentioned it in 50 years. Ever. In all those years, it just never came up. Talk about humility. I only learned about the medal the week he was dying. I was collecting some of his personal items and I asked him how he got it. My father told me that his plane was on a mission over Germany with several tons of bombs loaded and ready for deployment. When the doors were released for the bombs to drop, they did not open. They were frozen shut due to the high altitude at which the plane was flying. They quickly tried to reduce altitude in the hopes of thawing out the frozen door mechanism. The problem was that the bombs were on timers and were going to explode in seconds. My father jumped on the bombs and put all the pins back in each bomb. He also was sitting on top of the release door, which could have opened at any time, sending him down with the bombs. He got all the pins back in each bomb before they exploded, jumped off the hatch and saved his plane and all the crew members. No wonder they call his generation the "Greatest Generation."

Both of my parents lived within walking distance of work and they walked to work together every day. We ate dinner together as a family, always. After dinner we would play catch or play hockey or go fishing. My parents always had time for us, even when my dad worked two jobs to make ends meet. We lived in an actual neighborhood where people did not move every two years and we could actually tell you the names of all of our neighbors in a five-block radius. I still can tell you who lived there and all the family names more than 50 years later. I am still friends with all the neighborhood guys I grew up with. We sure do miss that today. We don't even have dinner together as families anymore. I think that is one of the most significant reasons that family members today become distant from one another.

Believe in Something Bigger Than You

When I learned that my dad's prostate cancer had returned and had spread to his bones and brain, I was devastated. I had to tell my mom that he had two weeks to live. He insisted on being brought home and we arranged for hospice care (which is staffed by angels in human form). As the cancer attacked my father's brain, it took away his ability to speak clearly and he could not write either, as his motor skills became progressively more impaired. Near the end, as I watched my father spiral downward, I realized that this was so much bigger than me. I was CEO of my own company, I had graduated from top business schools, I had money in the bank, I knew a lot of people and there were not many things that went on in my life that I couldn't influence or affect. But this was so far out of my league.

There was nothing I could do and I was totally helpless. All I could do was watch, pray and be there for his transition. That is why it is critical to believe in something bigger than you, that there must be a reason things happen the way they do, there must be a grand plan and something beyond this life.

As sick as he was, a few days before he died, my father was like his old self. He was laughing and he talked about his life and his days in the service and old times and the memories we had together. I had always heard it is not uncommon that just before people die they get a rush of energy and become fully aware. Many medical professionals will tell you that this is a sign that the end is very near. That is what happened to my dad, and I call this time of clarity "God's window." I believe that there are times when God gives you one last chance to connect and to have one last memory with your loved ones. One last time to see them as you always knew them. I remember asking him if he was scared. I didn't say "scared of dying," but he knew exactly what I meant. He looked at me directly in the eyes and said, "No, Gary, I am not scared. I lived a great life and got 10 more years of life than I thought I would because I caught my prostate cancer early. I have no regrets. I married the girl of my dreams and have beautiful children whom I am very proud of. It is my time and I know that you will take care of your mom after I am gone."

What I was most thankful for was the fact that I had no bridges to repair with him, no things left unsaid, and no regrets. My dad knew I loved him and I knew he loved me because we showed each other that every day. My mom and dad were always included in my life and I showed them how important they were to me every day. I can't imagine how people who lose loved ones and have unresolved issues with them are able to carry on. I cannot think of a worse thing to have to live with for the rest of your life. I wish that burden on no one. If you have unresolved issues with loved ones, please do not wait until they are dying to mend your relationship. You might not get the chance later and living with that pain is far worse than having to suck it up and swallow your ego to repair the damage long before it's too late. Make this a priority in your life. Watching my father die was the most difficult thing I had to face up to that point in my life. It was also the most powerful thing that ever happened to me because I grew enormously as a person from his passing. I learned that it is essential to believe in something bigger than you because something far bigger was at play in that room the day he passed.

I also learned not to take any day for granted. My dad would have given everything he owned for two more days with his wife. We tend to take our days for granted until we don't have many left. I always wondered why it takes trauma, a devastating life event or even close calls with death before we even think about living every day to its fullest. If you were told you had two weeks to live, how would you spend that time? What would you do differently? Why not do that now?

A philosopher once asked Alexander the Great, "What will you do next?" Alexander said, "I want to conquer Asia Minor."

"Then what?" the philosopher asked.

"Then I will unite Greece, then conquer Persia…" and on and on Alexander went. The philosopher asked him, "What will you do when there are no more countries to conquer?" Alexander the Great said, "I will come back and relax, play with my children, work on my garden and enjoy my life."

The philosopher's final question to Alexander was, "Why can't you just do that now?"

After my father died, my mother was completely lost. The following year was a tough one for us all. My brother went to rehab, I went through my divorce, and my mother was there for us all the way. Later that year we straightened out our lives. My brother came out of rehab and was doing well, and I had completed my divorce and bought a new place to live and my business was doing well. My mom spent that Christmas at my house and we had a great time. We even convinced her to take a puff from a hookah pipe I had brought back from Egypt. At our big Christmas Eve party, we laughed, danced and sang carols with the whole family, just like old times. We stayed up late and talked about everything. At some point during the evening my mom sat down in a rocking chair and just looked around, smiling. She was enjoying seeing all of her kids happy for the first time in a while. She began talking to our great family friend, Peter. She told him that it made her happy to see all her children doing well. Now she could go and be with my father.

Thirteen days later she passed away. I got a call from my sister saying that I had better get to Mom's house because she was sick and might not make it. My sister is a nurse and had worked with dying patients for years. She knew this was not good. My mom had a pancreatic aneurism, one of only seven recorded cases in medical history in the United States at that time. Just prior to being rushed to the hospital, my mother told my sister that she was in bed experiencing severe pain—bleeding and scared—and she looked up and saw my father standing at the foot of her bed. He told her that everything was going to be all right. He told her he would not let anything hurt her and that he was there to take her. I did not learn that until after she had passed away. At 3 a.m., my mother went into cardiac arrest and the doctors made us leave the room while they went into life-saving procedures or "code blue," as they call it. Then I was asked to make a decision that no one thinks will ever happen to them. The doctors asked me if I wanted them to stop working on my mother or to continue. Her vital signs were faint and fading fast. They don't ask you that question unless it is past the point of recovery. No matter what school you attend or what advanced degree you earn, or how much training you have received at your job, never does anyone teach you how to act in a situation like this. My father had come for her and she was ready to go. I could not stand in the way of their wanting to spend eternity together. I asked for the doctors to give me one last read of her vital signs and my decision was clear. "You have to stop now," I told the doctor. My sister knew all along what the right decision was, but to her credit she knew that I had to decide for myself and come to terms with it or it would haunt me forever. She was right.

For our Christmas presents that year, my mother had handwritten three small books for each of her children that contained all the family recipes we loved so we could carry on those traditions with our families. She also wrote extensively about how much she loved us, how much we meant to her and how her life was complete.

My mom was married twice. Her first husband was killed in an industrial accident when my brother and sister were very young. Years later, she met and married my father to whom she was married for more than 50 years. She told us how much she loved them, how happy they were together, how much they loved us. She told us what kind, decent and loving people they were. She wanted us to know and appreciate them the way she had and for us to know them as deeply as she did. She wrote about the type of men our fathers were and how they met, their lives together, and all the things that we never knew or asked about. She told us about how much they both meant to her. Stories only she could tell of those years before we were born. This was her final gift to us, and it was the best gift she could give us. My mom knew this was going to be her last Christmas, and she knew she was going home to be with my father. She knew. It all made sense to me then. So when I say that it is important to believe in something bigger than you, believe it. I do for sure. This belief will be the only thing that you will have to comfort you and it will allow you to become stronger in the face of any adversity.

CHAPTER THREE

Good Goes Around

"I may not remember what you said,
I may not remember what you did,
But I will never forget how you made me feel."

—Maya Angelou

"Being a better giver makes you a better getter."

—Russell Simmons

One of the most amazing phenomenons I have discovered over the years is that "Good Goes Around." I have personally experienced it. When you do good things for people it comes back to you, as long as you don't give to get. Some people give for show. That does not work. But when you truly do nice things for others and expect nothing in return, you become richer in many ways. As Randy Pausch said, "If you live your life properly, the dreams will come to you."

Practice Acts of Kindness

I have always felt that my professional and life successes were a gift and that the reason I was afforded these successes is that I always give back. I know it sounds crazy, but it is true. When we go out to dinner as a family, we always pick a table of strangers and buy them dinner or lunch. Oftentimes, I let my kids select the table and the group that we target to buy dinner for. The only requirement we have is that they cannot be told who it was that bought their meal and that the restaurant cannot take credit for it. I want people to know and believe that there are still good people out there and show them how it feels to be the beneficiary of a random act of kindness. Maybe, just maybe, they will pass it along with an act of their own kindness. It is amazing to see how far kindness goes with people. I have a vacation home in Upstate New York and spend a lot of time there. One night my son and I were in a restaurant that we frequent and I was talking with a person at the bar about his volunteer work with military veterans. He was a very nice guy who spent his days making sure that all the veterans in the area had food, clothes and were taken care of, at his own expense. We talked about his unselfishness, and I told him how much I respected his actions. He mentioned that people in this area are extremely nice and concerned about others. He then told me a story of a guy who lives somewhere on a private lake nearby who randomly buys people food and dinners all across the area. He went on to say how the entire town talks about the mysterious man who buys these dinners and how it makes everyone feel good to know people were out there who did these types of things. My son and I both looked at each other. I smiled because that person he was talking about was me. It was funny how far these simple acts had carried and the effect they had on this small town.

One time I anonymously bought dinner for a group of World War II veterans who were gathered at a hotel for a reunion of their military unit. Even more remarkable, they were part of a special group of veterans who had all been awarded Purple Hearts for being wounded in action. The veterans were with their spouses and when I learned of this reunion, I asked the general manager of the hotel to bring me their entire bill. I told the manager not to tell the veterans who paid for their meal, but just to thank them for their service to our country.

They were in the dining room of the hotel, and my friend and I were in the bar area. The bar was packed, so I was sure they would have no idea who paid for their group's bill. All of a sudden, I looked up and about 10 of the veterans, all in their late 70s or early 80s, came storming into the bar, as much as 80-years-olds can storm anyway. The group was led by a small, stout guy who called out to the entire bar, "All right, who did it? Who did it!?!? We want to know who paid for our dinners and drinks."

I thought, "Yikes, they look angry." Maybe they were too proud to accept this type of act and were offended. I also was thinking that I was going to get my butt kicked by a bunch of 80-year-olds. The entire bar had gone silent as the veterans continued to shout, "We want to know who did this—who bought us dinner?"

It was time to face the music. If they wanted to be mad, then I needed to let them vent at the right guy. So I stood up and said, "I did that."

They all stopped in their tracks and gathered around me in a circle. The leader said, "So it was you?" I swallowed hard and said, "Yes." He turned and shouted, "I found him, this is the guy."

Then about 10 more guys came in with their wives, so the crowd grew larger and the bar was now fully engaged in whatever was going to happen. It is bad enough to get beat up by 70- to 80-year-old guys, but now it looked like their wives wanted to smack me too. Looking around at them all, I stammered that the reason I paid for their dinners was to offer a small gesture of respect and appreciation for all they had done for our country. I told them that my father was a World War II veteran and I was very proud of him and of all those who served. This packed bar on a Saturday night went completely silent. Then something amazing happened. The leader stepped forward and embraced me in the biggest hug anyone could give. The entire bar broke out in applause and gave the veterans a standing ovation. The rest of the night was awesome as the veterans and their wives all took turns hugging me, and we spent the rest of the evening with those veterans as they told us some of the most fantastic stories from their war experiences that I ever heard. It was a magical night.

Being a Better Giver Makes You a Better Getter

I know that good goes around. When I first started my own business, The Summit Group, which is a high-end sales-training and consulting firm, I had to work hard to get it going. Long hours, head down. For relief I used to run in my neighborhood to burn off the stress. I remembered that as I ran, I would often pass a woman who was also running in my neighborhood and would casually say hello to her as we passed. One day there was a knock on my door and it was the woman whom I would see when I ran. She was surprised to see me, but went on to tell me that she was running in an event to raise money for a family in town whose 6-year-old son had been diagnosed with leukemia. The family was taking him to Boston for treatment and could not afford the lodging necessary for the parents to stay in Boston for the extended period of time required to complete their son's treatment. She asked if I would be interested in sponsoring her and pledging money to support her cause. I looked at her and asked how much was needed to ensure that this family would have all of their expenses covered. She told me how much it would cost and for whom she was raising the money. "Wait, I'll be right back," I said.

I don't know why, but something struck me and I came back with a check for the entire amount. The woman was floored. She could not believe that someone she barely knew had done this. I told her that I thought what she was doing was fantastic and that I was glad I could help. Later that night I received a call from the father of the child who had leukemia. The father was crying and he told me how incredible it was that someone had done something like this for his family. He was shocked that a complete stranger would help out his family and thanked me a million times over. That was a phone call I will never forget.

One month later, as I was still trying to get my business off the ground and looking for that one big deal, that one big break I needed to launch my company, I received a phone call from a potential client who represented one of the largest utility companies in the United States. The woman was the director of training for Southern California Edison and we began talking about her training needs for the company and what we could do to support them. We talked for about 50 minutes and the conversation went very well. As we were concluding the call, she said, "So this is ABC Company, right?" I said, "No, you called The Summit Group." She stopped and said, "You are kidding me. I was calling for the ABC Company. I must have dialed the wrong number by mistake and got your company. But it doesn't matter now because I really liked what you had to say so we will do business with you."

What are odds of not only dialing a wrong number, but getting another sales-training company? Even still, getting a sales-training company with the same area code as the one you are dialing. Also, she never asked the name of my company until the very end of the call. Had she done that in the beginning, she probably would have just said, "I am sorry," hung up and redialed. That contract ended up being seven figures and launched my company. The Summit

Group went on to become one of the most successful and highly regarded sales-training companies in the world in our specialty of value creation. All due to a wrong number. I truly believe that it was no random act. One month earlier I helped that family whose son had leukemia; you cannot tell me the two are unrelated. This was a clear example of how being a better giver makes you a better getter, as long as you don't give to get. Here is a good rule to live by: Always give without remembering and receive without forgetting.

Beware of the Takers

Now let me tell you about another type of person. Many people in this world are takers. That is what they do. They disguise themselves in many ways and do it so well that you may never know they are takers until it is too late. They not only show no gratitude at all, but if given the chance will intentionally take advantage of you and the situation. There are also tremendous people out there who never show you how good they truly are. As they say, still waters run deep. Either way, people will always do something that reveals their true DNA. Good and bad. If you pay close attention you will see it, and once you do, make no mistake about it, that is who they truly are. That is not to say that one cannot ever change, but it usually takes a significant emotional event in their lives to do so. Ebenezer Scrooge changed but he had the help of three ghosts on Christmas Eve (four if you count Jacob Marley).

On the good side, I have an acquaintance, Craig Ludwig, who currently does a radio show for the NHL Dallas Stars hockey club. He won two Stanley Cups, one with the Montreal Canadians and the other with the Dallas Stars. When I met Craig's father for the very first time, he was wearing his son's first Stanley Cup ring from his Montreal team. I asked him about the ring and he said his son gave it to him because without all the sacrifices his father made for him, he would have never won it. That's why Craig gave the ring to his dad. He didn't even know if he would ever win again; many players don't win once, much less twice, in a lifetime. When I heard that story, I knew immediately who this guy was and what he was all about. Class act. I have a childhood friend who gave up being able to move outside of our hometown so he could take care of his ailing mother who was sick with cancer. I don't need to know anymore about him than that. Class act.

On the other side, people's actions can reveal their not-so-nice sides, their dark sides. I don't care how much they try to camouflage them-selves with nice clothes, charity work, their circle of so-called friends, Bible-study classes, big houses and whatever else, they too will always do something that shows you who they really are at their very core. Even though you may not want to believe it, that is them, period. Once you read those tea leaves, then you can decide what level of relationship you want to have with them. You can see where the danger spots are and step around them or cut them loose entirely.

Let me give you an example of this that I experienced. I was flying back from a business trip with an associate who worked for me in my training company. We had always gotten along well and he was a smart guy, so I didn't see the signs. I should have caught it earlier. In this case we were flying back from a client meeting and it was late. I had three million miles on Delta Air Lines and usually was afforded a first-class upgrade every time I flew. He had a lot of miles as well, but I had travel seniority by Delta standards. As it turned out, I was given the last first-class seat on the plane. I didn't think it was right for me to be in first class while my associate sat in coach. I went up to the gate agent and turned in my first-class seat and arranged to sit next to my associate in coach so that we could sit together on the long flight home.

Unknown to me, after I turned in my first-class upgrade, the gate agent offered the same seat to my associate because he was next in line in seniority. Not only did he *take* the first-class seat for himself, but he made fun of me for having to sit in coach. He was relentless: he implied how much more important he was than me and how much more clout he had with the airlines, and he laughed that he hoped I enjoyed sitting in a crowded coach class. What he didn't know was that the only reason he got that seat was because I gave it up so I could sit with him. I did not feel it would be right to upgrade myself, especially if he could not get an upgrade himself. He does not know to this day that his seat was a result of me giving mine up. I never told him because, really, what was the point? He had just taught me something very important about who he truly was as a person. This was a prime example of someone showing his true DNA. I took note of it and realized that he was someone whom I needed to be guarded around. I filed this knowledge away and continued to maintain the relationship with a very skeptical eye. As it turned out, years later he and his wife both did something so senseless and hurtful that it has severed our relationship completely and permanently. Lesson learned. Leopards don't change their spots, and you are better off without those types of people around you.

You will run into people who are takers in this world and they will fool you. The question becomes, do you stop being a giver? Do you let those instances where people cheat you, lie to you, take advantage of you or betray you in some way in the face of any graciousness they may receive change who you are? Those things can easily make you jaded and guarded. They may even make you say to yourself, "Well, I am not going to ever do that again." After a lot of hard thinking about this question, I have come to the conclusion that you cannot allow bad people to dictate the kind of person you are and who you want to be. If you do, they win. For sure, people will take from you and disappoint you in life. You will become smarter about reading people in the future and be more guarded, but you cannot allow them to determine who you are and who you become. Would I give up my first-class seat again to someone else for the same reasons? Yes, I would because that is who I am.

When a sex scandal broke around Oprah Winfrey's girls boarding school that she opened in South Africa for $40 million back in 2007, I am sure she was devastated. Oprah is a great woman who gives back more than anyone will ever realize, and she faced the ultimate betrayal for her efforts by one individual. To be fair, the woman who was accused of these sexual-abuse charges was found not guilty. Nine girls testified against the accused, but she was acquitted. While Oprah was disappointed in the outcome, as she said in a statement, I am sure she will not give up doing great things for people. Oprah is an excellent example of how you cannot let questionable or bad people change who you are and what you know is right.

I make it a priority in my life to practice acts of kindness to people. Here are some random acts of kindness that you can do with little difficulty:

- Baby-sit for a harried parent

- Donate your money or time

- Buy dinner for someone anonymously

- Hug someone who needs it

- Community service

- Send flowers, cards, or call someone to show you care

- Send a simple thank-you note to someone who made a difference in your life

It's not so much what you do; it is the attention and intention that people notice.

A World Champion Giver

So if you still think there are no random acts of kindness in life and you aren't convinced that Good Goes Around, I offer this final story, which was told to me by a remarkably bright and innovative man named Dan Migala. Dan is currently the vice president of creative partnerships for the San Diego Padres. We see each other every year at a major sports marketing event sponsored by another wonderful guy whom I am proud to call my friend, Mike Veeck. Both Dan and I are speakers at this event, which is held to honor Mike Veeck's dad, Bill Veeck and his creative genius.

One year at the event, Dan told me about a young college kid who was an intern for the Boston Red Sox in 2004, the year the Red Sox won the World Series for the first time in 86 years. After they won, the Red Sox—in connection with the Massachusetts State Lottery—toured several of the large shopping malls in the state with two or three players from the team and the championship trophy. Needless to say, the turnout at each event was huge. Long lines of people wanting pictures and autographs with their favorite players made it difficult to leave each venue and get to the next one on time. At one particular event, the Red Sox were really pressed for time and clearly not everyone in line was going to be able to meet the players. This young intern noticed a 12-year-old boy sitting on a bench, crying his eyes out. Of all the thousands of people in this mall, this young boy stood out, so the intern went over and asked the boy what was wrong. The little boy was upset that he was not going to be able to meet his favorite player, Jason Varitek, who was signing autographs that day. The boy said he had even skipped school that day to get there. The intern looked at the boy and said, "Wait here and I'll see what I can do." About 45 minutes later, he came back for the boy and took him on the bus with all the players, including Varitek. The boy got all the autographs and pictures he wanted. He left that bus walking on cloud nine.

Three months later that young man was at home after his internship had ended when the phone rang. It was a senior executive from the Red Sox. The kid had no idea that anyone above his immediate boss even knew he existed. The executive asked the young man to come into his office for a meeting. You can imagine how nervous he was because he had no idea what this was all about. Maybe he was in trouble. All kind of thoughts raced through his head.

When he got to the Red Sox head office, he sat down with the top Red Sox executive and another man at a large conference table. The man asked "Is this the kid? The Red Sox executive answered, "It sure is." The man looked at this young kid and said, "You don't know me, but do you remember a 12-year-old boy who was crying on a bench because he wasn't going to be able to meet his favorite player, Jason Varitek? You saw him and talked to him and then brought him on the team bus to meet the players. Do you remember that?" The intern said he did. "Well, that was my son, and the reason he was there to get Jason Varitek's autograph is that he was my wife's favorite player. My wife passed away earlier in the year and my son went there to see Varitek in memory of her."

The intern sat there stunned. That man was there to complete a substantial and long-term corporate sponsorship with the Red Sox and he told the Red Sox executive that he wanted this intern to receive 100 percent of any commissions for this deal. So this young college intern received all the commissions as a result of him being a great giver and doing something for someone without any expectation of anything in return.

With that, I rest my case. Good really does go around.

CHAPTER FOUR

Don't Major
in the Minors

"I'll be there when I get there and I'll stay until I'm gone."

—"Midnight" Mike Martin

Bartender extraordinaire, Old Forge, N.Y.

"You can be good on the broiler, but don't be too good on the broiler, because you'll always work the broiler."

—Bob Burnap

Assistant manager Burger King

(Where I worked the broiler
when I was 16 years old)

People are overwhelmed by the complexities of their own lives. Much of the problem is their own doing. Many people let their jobs consume them—jobs many people don't even enjoy, where they work for people they don't really like. Some people let their kids' lives consume them, trying to drive their kids to baseball, soccer, scouts, piano lessons, friends' houses, school and wherever else, and they become a full-time taxi for their kids. Is it a crime to spend time at home with your family? People even get wrapped up in having to go to different relatives' homes for the holidays. Christmas Eve with Dad and stepmom, Christmas morning with Mom and stepdad, Christmas brunch with the mother-in-law and her boyfriend, and Christmas evening dinner with the father-in-law and his wife. Then in our own lives we let little things develop into major things. We tend to focus our energies on things that ultimately mean nothing.

The secret of life is really very, very simple: Be Good and Do Good. That's it! The key is to simplify our lives and slow down. We all need to take a break and spend time with the truly important people in our lives. A small town in New Jersey actually mandated one day of the week where there would be no kids' sports or external activities so families could stop, catch their breath, and spend time together. It's incredible that a town would have to legislate a day for something as basic as making families slow down and spend time together. Don't get me wrong. I was wrapped up in this spin cycle just like everyone else I knew. I had three sons who all played hockey (sometimes 15 games a weekend), baseball, soccer, football and lacrosse. It was complete insanity. While I was going to all these games, I also had my own company and traveled often for work. No time for myself at all. It is pretty sad when your refuge becomes cutting the grass, but I had to make yard work a relaxing event because I had no time to relax doing anything else. My life had to change or I was going to implode.

Never Trade Life Worth for Net Worth

At this time, two events happened that became a turning point and inspired me to change my whole life and shift my priorities from acquiring net worth to focusing my energies on life worth. These two events are responsible for how I now live my life.

The first instance happened when I had finally had a weekend at home. However, instead of closing my office doors and not even thinking about work until Monday like any sane person would, I received a bid opportunity for my company, The Summit Group, to do a significant amount of sales training for Hewlett-Packard. I felt that I needed to respond to this bid request immediately. Even though the response date was 14 days away, I wanted to jump right into this project. When I think back on those days I want to kick myself. It really makes me sick to think of the time I lost doing things that didn't really matter. The truth was that I had enough time to respond to this bid during my regular work week. What's more, the real truth was that we really did not need the additional business at all. I was greedy and I wanted it all. What an idiot! It makes me shudder even writing about it now, especially in hindsight. So I began working on the response. Head down, here we go again.

After I had spent about four hours of a beautiful sunny Saturday working on this proposal, I heard a faint knock on my office door. I looked up and I saw my 12-year-old son standing there with two baseball mitts, a baseball and his baseball hat. His eyes looked around my office and at the computer where I had been pounding away. He said, "Dad, are you done yet? I have been waiting outside your door for you to finish so we could go outside and play catch."

I started to respond, "Well, I can't right now because I am in the middle of something and won't be done for a while," but as the last words rolled off my tongue, I saw the most devastated look on his face. He looked like someone had just taken out his heart and crushed it. Someone actually did. Me. My son turned around and began walking slowly out of my office with his head slumped down in disappointment. Suddenly it was like someone had smacked me on the head. What was I doing? Are you kidding me? Was I going to sacrifice a day playing baseball with my son for Hewlett-Packard? (No offense HP, but my son comes first.) I called out to him and said, "You know what, let's play. I would rather play with you than work any day." My son's face was glowing. I still remember the look on his face and that was more than 20 years ago. I told myself: Never again would I do that, ever.

The next turning point in my life happened while I was on a trip to Spain. I was going to deliver the keynote speech for a sales event for Motorola. I had been working 14-hour days for three months, and I remember that when I got to the airport I was not feeling well. Early signs of the flu. Stupidly, I decided that I had to get on that plane. Why? Because I believed the world would cave in if I did not show up. What a tragedy it would be if I did not show up for a 45-minute talk! I also believed that no one would ever understand that I was sick and that there was no way Motorola could cover 45 minutes of time at the event. (In truth, they had hundreds of executives who could step in and talk in my place.) I had to go to Spain no matter how badly I felt, no question. So I got on that plane.

Any energy I had left was sucked out of me when the normally nine-hour flight became a 19-hour ordeal with delays and mechanical issues. When I arrived in Spain I was nearly delirious. I remember getting to my hotel room and being unable to sleep the whole night. Two full days without sleep on a body that was already failing. Running on pure vapors, I gave the talk at 8 a.m. the next morning. I don't remember giving the talk at all. I couldn't tell you what I said or anything about that event at all, even to this very day. I was like a zombie. What I do remember is getting back to my room. I don't know what a nervous breakdown is or what it feels like, but I think I probably had one right there. I remember crying and shaking uncontrollably because my body had given out both physically and emotionally. In that hotel room in Spain I realized that I was killing myself. And for what? For money? For one more client name on my roster of customers? I knew in my bones that if I did not draw the line right there, right then, I would ruin every part of my life that mattered to me. That is when I realized that I was majoring in the minors. In the cosmic totality of life, missing this event meant nothing. It was not a problem, but I made it a problem. Brain cancer is a problem, but this was not brain cancer. This was a 45-minute talk that most people would not remember an hour after they heard it. I put that before my health and common sense. Fortunately, that was when I learned two things that changed my life: the power of "NO" and the power of perspective.

The Power of "No"

When I first started my business I never said, "No." If a company wanted to do business with my company and wanted me to personally deliver the training, I said, "Yes." That was fine when I had eight clients, but when I had 20 clients it became much harder on me. When I had 50 clients, it was impossible. Sometimes the client would say, "We will do business with you, but you have to deliver the training or no deal." I'd think, "Well, I had better do what they say." After my experience in Spain I vowed this was going to stop. Nothing was worth risking my health again or taking me away from my family again. So when I got the next call from a customer who said we want only you to do this training or no deal, I said I cannot do that. I said that I could do the first class, but then I would hand off the training to my company's team of expert facilitators. I was not going to commit to doing all the training. An amazing thing happened: that company still did business with us. As time went on, I told more clients that I would not be doing any of the deliveries for them. And they still said, "OK."

One time a company asked me to give a keynote talk for them on a day that happened to be my son's birthday, I told them "No" and explained that I had a conflict. Guess what? The company reworked its schedule so that I could still deliver that speech. The power of "No" was and still is very liberating.

After seeing how it improved my professional life, I applied the power of "No" to other parts of my life. When people asked me over to parties or events that previously I would have felt obligated to attend, I said "No" because I wouldn't give up a Saturday with my kids. Where in the past I had to do the "Holiday Shuffle" and go to multiple homes so I wouldn't hurt anyone's feelings, I said "No" and invited everyone to come over to my home for the holidays. Or when I would go back to my hometown while on vacation and everyone would say, "Come over to our place," they mean well, but you wind up spending your entire vacation just traveling all around to visit relatives and friends and not having any time for your own vacation. I said, "No." Instead, I told those relatives and friends, "Here is where I will be and here is the time period when I will be there. You come see me." If they didn't, then they must not have wanted to see me too badly. Learn and use the power of "No." It will unburden your life tenfold.

The Power of Perspective

The other thing I learned is the "Power of Perspective." It is hugely important in getting your life back on track and lessening your burdens. Most of the time the things we think are problems in our lives are not problems at all. In many cases, we lose perspective about how good we really have it or we lose sight of the fact that many others have much worse issues to deal with. We should be mindful of the difficulties others face when we find ourselves whining over something goofy or trivial.

I am a faculty member and lecture at several major corporations' executive-leadership programs. MARRIOTT International and Ritz-Carlton (owned by MARRIOTT) are just two of the companies of which I am proud to be part of their faculty team. I want to talk about these two companies because to me MARRIOTT and Ritz-Carlton are tremendously people-centric organizations and truly care about their people inside the workplace and outside of the workplace. They are more than clients to me, they are my friends. The people who work there are some of the nicest and kindest people I know and the MARRIOTT family is unparalleled in how they run their business and how they make a difference in people's lives. They are the only company I know that actually provides a training class for their employees on how to create personal value in their lives. I developed this program especially for them and I teach it personally because it changes people's lives.

One of the exercises in this class is centered on teaching the executives the "power of perspective." I ask them to identify something in their lives they experience that really makes them upset, something that drives them crazy so much so that it can affect their entire day, week or month. I am not talking about social issues like child abuse—everyone gets upset at that. I mean things like being cut off in traffic, or being taken advantage of, or being misled or lied to, things like that. Once the executives in my class identify these things that irritate them, I ask them to describe how they feel about it and why. Some people get visibly angry just talking about these things.

After everyone is finished venting about what really gets under their skin, I tell them that I am going to teach them the power of perspective. Then I play a video set to music that shows photos of children who have lost their battles with terminal cancer. The video is about three minutes long and as the executives watch pictures of these wonderful children, tears begin to stream down their faces. The room goes deadly silent. You could hear a pin drop as each person comes to understand how ridiculous it is for them to let such trivial things as being cut off in traffic consume them. They realize that the issues they identified earlier as things that upset their day or even their whole week are so minor and insignificant. Many of them are ashamed that they allowed those things any time in their lives at all, especially when watching a video of children who have passed away from cancer. After the video stops I ask them one simple question: "So how important are those things now?" Lesson learned.

The small speed bumps in life that used to upset me are almost non-existent now. If something starts to bother me, I always ask myself, is this really a problem? If I had one month to live, would this even be on my radar screen? I do the same thing at work as well. I do not mean to sound flippant at all here, but it is only a job. When I was in sales my goal was to make my numbers and be home in time for dinner with my kids.

My oldest son Dan works in the medical field as a medical sales consultant for doctors and surgeons. A major part of his job is spent in the operating rooms observing surgeries. We talk often about the sales end of his business. Since I am an expert in sales by profession and the company I founded trains the sales forces of the top companies in the world to sell more effectively, my son often asks my advice on his sales efforts. I remember one day in particular when he was very nervous about meeting that month's sales quota. He asked me questions like, how could he close the gap? What could he do to drive sales? What would his boss say? How would this affect his career? Talk about déjà vu. These were the exact same things that I would have lost sleep over 30 years ago when I first started in my career. I know better now. After we talked and I offered my son advice, we made plans to talk later in the week to see how he was progressing.

When we connected later that week, my son seemed a bit different. That sense of urgency was no longer there. I asked him, what had happened? He said he just came out of surgery that day after observing two "open and close" cases. I asked what that term meant. He said that an open-and-close case means that the surgeons open up the patients during surgery, look around and find that there is nothing more that can be done, and then simply close them back up. He told me that both cases were people under the age of 35. One of them went in for a bowel resection and when they opened him up they found his entire body was covered with cancer. He was terminal and had just weeks to live. My son said, "Dad, I saw his wife in the waiting room, she had two small children, she had no idea that her life was about to be turned upside down." I asked him how he felt about that. He was sad and shaken up. These people were his age. He has a wife and two children. He hesitated and then said he learned that his sales quota was really not that important. What he learned was the power of perspective.

To be clear, I am NOT suggesting that you don't give a full effort at work. Quite the contrary. When you put things into perspective, you free yourself to perform better at work and at home. I always believe that you are at your very best when your life is in harmony and when you are happy with your whole life. The ideas in this book are ways to find that harmony and I know they work because they worked for me.

Your Calling Is Out There—Find It!

The final concept I want to share about majoring in the minors is the notion of finding your calling. Find what it is that you are meant to do and that is what you should do. I always tell people when I speak to them that it is so important to find what it is they love to do and do that. The reason is that if you are doing what you truly love, then your chances of being successful and making significant contributions are 10 times better than if you just do any random job or go down any arbitrary career path. Second, if you are doing what you truly love to do, you will be ahead of 98 percent of the people I know. Either way, you have to find your calling. Everyone has a calling, something they are destined to do, something that the gifts and talents they have been given are supposed to be used for.

In her book, *Mother Teresa In Her Own Words*, she tells of the many people who would contact her and offer themselves to travel to Calcutta to help her do her work with the sick and the poor. She would always give them the same reply. She would say, "Stay where you are. Find your own Calcutta. Find the sick, the suffering and the lonely right where you are- in your own homes and in your own families, in your workplaces and in your schools." What she was saying was look around you, you can find your calling if you have eyes to see. If you seek to help people in need as your calling, you have no need to look beyond the very place where you live. There is an old saying, "Only the dumbest of mice would ever hide behind a cat's ear, but only the smartest of cats would ever think to look there." Often times, the things we seek most are right under our noses (or behind our ears, as this saying goes) and we will never see them if we don't look.

To jump into a place meant for someone else without fully under-standing your true calling will never fulfill you. Some people are meant to work with the sick, some to work with children, some are meant to teach, some are meant to move people through music, but make no mistake, everyone has a calling. The most frequent question I get is, how do you find your calling? I always answer the same way: you don't find your calling, your calling finds you. But you have to be available and open. Events happen in our lives for very specific reasons. People come in and out of lives for very specific reasons, good and bad. I really believe that. As I said earlier in this book, there are no random acts. Things cross our paths and provide us with experiences designed to prepare us for whatever it is we are supposed to become in our lives.

To enhance your chances of finding your calling, you must be available and open. This means to not only be aware, but also to allow yourself opportunities to try new and different things so you can expand your hopes of finding what you truly love to do and what you are meant to do. Keep in mind that there is a huge difference between what you want to "Be" and what you want to "Do" in life. An important distinction, for sure. You might say you want to "Be" a manager in a company, but do you want to "Do" what managers have to do? Do you like having to fire people? Do you like having to write 15 performance reviews, one for each employee? Do you like telling some of your people they are not cutting it and have to be placed on probation and won't be getting their raise this year? Those are things you have to do that go with what you want to be.

The "Buffet" Table

I remember once speaking to about 200 college kids in Clemson University's marketing program. I asked them to raise their hands if they planned on going into the field of marketing once they graduated. All hands were raised. Then I said, "So you all are dedicating these four years of college to prepare you for a career in the profession of marketing, is that right?" Yes, for sure, they said. I said, "Well, let's assume that the average career length is about 25 years—could be 30 years—but let's stay with 25. So you have decided that not only will you dedicate these four years of college to the field of marketing but you are prepared to give 25 more years of your lives to this as well. So that is a total of 29 years that you are planning to allot for this career." They still said yes, but a little less emphatically this time. "OK," I said. "The final question I have for you is this, can anyone name for me four jobs titles in the field of marketing and what those job titles do?" Thundering silence. "OK, name me three." Again nothing. Does anyone besides me see how nuts this is? You are telling me that you are going to dedicate nearly 30 years of your life to a profession where you can't even name three job titles or tell me what those jobs do? Talk about running blind. It's not their fault, but my point is that if you do not try different things you will never get the wealth of experience from which to make sound decisions regarding your life path, nor will you find your calling. It's funny, but I find most people put more thought into planning their vacations than they do in planning their own lives.

I like to use the "Buffet Table" analogy when I speak about how to find your calling. Imagine a large buffet table filled with food but each dish is covered so you cannot see what food is underneath. Then I tell you to pick one of those dishes and whatever food is under there, that is the food you have to eat for the next 25 years. Would that be OK with you? Of course not. Wouldn't you rather try as many of those dishes as you could to see which food you really liked first and THEN decide? You bet. But we don't do that with our careers or our lives. My point is that it is important to take risks and try different things. You cannot get struck by lightning without going out into the rain. Finding your calling and doing what you truly love to do means that you have to be unafraid to take chances and make changes if something is not meant for you to do. Your calling is out there. Be available and ready and your calling will find you, but it helps if you meet it halfway.

CHAPTER FIVE

Relationship Refinement: "Thinning the Herd"

"I don't talk to you because I don't like you,
I never did like you, and I am never going to
like you, so just stay away from me."

–My Dad, Frank Kunath

*(To a fellow worker at a family
gathering for union workers)*

"Dimmi Chi Frequenti, E Ti Diro' Chi Sei."

–Old Italian Saying

*Translation: "Tell me who you hang around
with and I will tell you who you are."*

A key ingredient to achieving a high life worth is to surround yourself with great people. People you truly care about and, here is the key, people who truly care about you. I know it sounds like an obvious statement, but what is not obvious is, how do you figure out who those people are? What you will find is that ultimately far fewer of those great people exist and you will go through many relationships with many people before you figure out who are the ones that are true-blue friends. The 1 percenters, as I call them. These are people who care as much or more about you and others as they do about themselves. People who are genuinely happy for your successes and not conditionally happy based on the fact that they are happy for you as long your successes do not exceed their own.

The quote that I used from my father for this chapter heading comes from when I was 9 years old. We were at a family gathering for the union workers at Bendix Aerospace Corporation, where my father was a tool and die maker, a very skilled trade. Some guy kept trying to talk to my father, but my father would not give him the time of day. Finally out of frustration, the guy said, "Hey, Frank, I keep trying to talk to you but you keep ignoring me, how come?" My dad simply turned to the guy and said, "I don't talk to you because I don't like you and I never will." I was shocked that he was so blunt. Later, I asked my father, "Why did you talk like that to that guy?" He simply said, "I really don't like him, he is not a good person and I don't want those types of people around me. I thought that he should know that up front and now he knows." At that time I thought it was a bit harsh, but now as I look back on that event with all my life experiences, I see it as pure genius. Yes, it was a bit harsh and could have been said more diplomatically, but the genius was in my father's recognition that you need to cut people out of your life who do not add value to your life.

There are four types of people I have found: energy "gainers," energy "drainers," takers and the 1 percenters. Energy "drainers" are people who intentionally or unintentionally suck the life force out of you. People who make you feel worse after they leave than you did before they came. People whom you dread being around. Energy "drainers"are a chore. They deplete you much like a "sucker" branch on a tomato plant, those branches that take the nutrients from the plant but will never bear any fruit. Earlier in this book, I mentioned that there are "takers" and "givers" in life. Unfortunately there are many more takers than givers. Takers are energy "drainers." Takers take, that is what they do. I call them human "remoras." Remoras are those little fish that ride free under a shark's mouth. The remoras let the sharks do all the work in catching food and they simply feed off the efforts of the shark.

You'll often find it difficult to figure out who is who, but it is critical to do so. Your life worth depends on it. Takers are very good at hiding who they are because it makes it easier for them to take when the chance materializes. In fact, sometimes takers don't even know they are takers until an opportunity presents itself. For example, when a family member passes away and the family needs to divide up the assets. That is when takers rise and show themselves. You see the worst come out in some people. Another example is when you loan people money or support them in some way, maybe letting them live with you through a tough time or letting them borrow your car, or when you go into business with them and the first dollar rolls in. These things will illuminate the differences between the takers and the 1 percenters.

The key to a high life worth is to develop a circle of people who are 1 percenters and who are also energy "gainers" to your life. I have been burned many times in my life when I have misread people. I thought they were something that they were not and their actions later revealed their true DNA. It is especially difficult when you want to give people the benefit of the doubt because you open yourself up a bit. As part of my business, we commonly have relationships with other firms to help deliver training around the world. While most of these firms are honorable and great to work with, I had a "not so nice" experience with one of them. My company had an arrangement where we would use this firm to do some international deliveries for our customers that we could not economically serve. We introduced this firm to several of our clients with whom they had no relationship at all and we taught them how to deliver our training material, which was protected by copyright and trademark laws. It was considered intellectual property that was owned by my company. What we later found out was that, unknown to us, they had taken our training content—altered a word or two to get around copyright infringement, but used our exact concepts and examples—and created their own program. They then doubled back and tried to sell it to our clients that we had introduced them to earlier. They even tried to undercut us on price. They did this all without our knowledge and while still smiling to our faces and playing the loving-partner card. I quickly severed that relationship. A total misread on my part. The signs were there, but I ignored them because I wanted to believe the best. I was wrong.

Four Ways to Distinguish the 1 Percenters From the Takers

Fortunately, identifying takers and 1 percenters isn't purely a guessing game. Here is a good way that I learned to assess people so I don't get burned. This framework was shared with me by a former business associate which I modified for my use. Is it foolproof? No, but it is pretty good. When I meet a person with whom I might have a personal or professional relationship, I look at four areas to figure out who a person truly is and read their core DNA.

No. 1: How Do They Speak of Themselves

The first thing I look at is how a person speaks of himself or herself. It tells me a lot about who they truly are as a person. Do they have a "Me first" mentality or a "You first" mentality? Are they humble or boastful? I am always more impressed with people who have done some pretty amazing things but don't talk about them. You only hear about their accomplishments when you talk with others. Still waters really do run deep. Listening to someone talk about themselves you also can find out the answers to questions like, do they hold a grudge or are they forgiving? What is the balance of listening versus talking? I find that the people who talk the most always have the least to say.

No. 2: How They Treat People and Things They Don't Need

The second thing I look at is how they treat people and things they don't need. How do they treat kids, their parents, senior citizens, waiters/waitresses and service staff, relatives, etc.? I was having dinner once at an acquaintance's home with his family and his 14-year-old son was talking very disrespectfully to his parents. I could not believe what I was hearing. He was even using foul language toward them. They tried to shrug it off by saying, "Oh that's just our little Timmy, he is very opinionated." I thought, "Opinionated? This kid's going to be in prison soon. You better fix this kid before he robs me in five years." I also look at how people treat pets or animals. That tells me a lot about them.

No. 3: Look at Their Friends

The third thing I look at is their friends. Tell me the people you hang around with and I will tell you who you are. Also what kind of friendships do they have? Convenient or unconditional? Are they an outsider trying to constantly validate themselves or impress others for some form of acceptance? Do they have long-term relationships or short-term ones? Many friends or a few?

No. 4: How Do They Spend Their Money

The final thing I observe is how they spend their money. People illuminate what they truly value through how they spend their money. If their kids have no diapers, but they bet football games, something is not right. Do they buy things or experiences? Are they impulsive or thoughtful? Is their fridge full of beer or formula?

Once you better understand the person deep down, you are in a position to decide just how close you want your relationship to be with this person and what level of trust you can place in him or her. I will say that I have learned as many things from the bad apples as I have from the great people. You can learn from anyone. I am always evaluating people and when it makes sense, trying to extract the things I like best about them and maybe even incorporating those things into my own life. On the flip side I take knowledge from the bad eggs too. Meeting those people allows me to set boundaries for myself about the type of person I never want to be. It sometimes helps to feel the impact of a taker or an energy "drainer," so you know what it feels like firsthand. That way you know that you will never want to do that to others.

There are also "Cactus Pear" people. Cactus pears are very prickly on the outside, but very flavorful and enjoyable on the inside once you get past the thorny exterior. Some people are just like that. Maybe it takes a little longer to figure them out, but they are often worth the wait. All I care about is who you truly are at your core. Where is your heart? No one is perfect and we all have our bad days and our dark sides. I can be fine with someone when I know that their heart is in the right place and that down deep they are a 1 percenter even if their exterior is a bit rough. As long as you are a 1 percenter, then I want you around me because I know you will be there for me unconditionally for the long haul.

Practice "Relationship Refinement"

Great relationships genuinely matter and they are a core component of having a high life worth. One of the things I do that is very important is something I call "Relationship Refinement." Every year I identify several relationships that are important to me and that I have been neglectful of. Then I list actions that I am going to take to revitalize those relationships. And I do it. Those are some of most rewarding relationships in my life today. Some people say they don't have the time to invest in rekindling relationships that they may have neglected. They want to, but always place it on a back burner. The truth is that it is not a time issue at all, it is a priority issue. Remember, you always have time to do the things you do first. I also hear people say, "The reason I don't contact them is that they never tried to reconnect with me." Who cares who makes the first move? That has no bearing on anything. Step up and make that call because you might miss out on a relationship that will change your life for good.

I also pick one or two relationships that I need to divest myself of entirely or at the very minimum, cut down significantly the amount of time and energy I spend on them. These can be friends, but it also applies to family.

The final thought on this topic is about who we are and how we act. Why would anyone want to be great friends with us? Are we 1 percenters? Are we energy "gainers?" One thing I can tell you is that as you gain more happiness in your life and improve your life worth, you will be sought out by others. The higher your comfort level is with your life, the more it allows you to just be yourself. People are attracted to authentic and happy people. People who are comfortable in being who they are and have no reason to be something or someone they are not. Just think of someone you find most enjoyable to spend time with. I bet it is someone who is authentic and happy. Young children are very authentic. They don't know how to be anything other than who they are. They are honest and take pleasure in simple things. Their hearts and intentions are pure. The same with many senior citizens, they have lived their lives and have seen it all. Have you ever been to a gathering where people watch the 80-year-old dancing or laughing up a storm? People naturally migrate to those folks because they exude a life force that attracts people to them like moths to a light. It is because they are authentic; they are themselves because after all these years they know that who they are is pretty darn good.

Be Interested, Not Interesting

A former business associate of mine had a dad who said the secret to being a great friend is to "Be interested and *not* interesting." That's a great line. Have you ever met someone who has remarkable accomplishments or has an impressive title or has material wealth and never acts that way or even mentions it? And when you talk to them, you find out that they act just like normal people. Invariably, you always say, "Wow, that person is a regular person, you would never know that he or she has this or that." That stays with you. I have always found that when people start a conversation with who they are or what they have, it tells me two things. One is that they are not happy with who they truly are because if they were they would not be defining themselves with material things or titles. The second thing I think is that when someone does this they probably don't have what they say they have. If you have it, you never have to say it, people just know. Either way, being authentic not only relieves you of the burden of being someone else, but it is the ultimate differentiator. As Rick Warren, the author of *The Purpose Driven Life*, said "God made you an original, don't let yourself become a carbon copy."

You have no need to be anything other than who you already are. The key is to find out who you are. Besides, the most important aspect of personal growth is not becoming more powerful, but becoming more human.

CHAPTER SIX

Life Is Fun and Fun Is Good

"Cause of Death: Life."

—Washington Post writer Thomas Boswell's epitaph
for legendary baseball man Bill Veeck

"The idea is to die young, as late as possible."

–Ashley Montagu

"I don't want to be rocking in a chair on my
porch when I am 80 years old saying I wished I
had, I want to be saying I'm glad I did."

–Gary Kunath

(Hey, it's my book so I can use
a quote or two of mine)

I try not to do anything nowadays that is not fun. If it isn't fun and I can't make it fun, then I don't want to do it. Most of the time, I can make anything fun. Are there things in life that are not going to be fun? For sure, but my thought is that if you have fun in every other part of your life, then when you *have* to do something that isn't fun, those past fun times will get you through it. I am not saying you should be a clown all the time, but I am saying that if you follow all the lessons in this book, your life will lighten up tremendously and you can start to have fun. Fun is a mindset. What is wrong with people having fun? Nothing.

The concept of fun applies to work as well. We all have plenty of opportunities to elevate our level of enjoyment and have fun at work, but we don't take advantage of them. Why? Because some people take things too seriously. When I worked for AT&T, I tried to make every job I had fun. Sometimes making the job fun was hard work, but if you don't try to embrace the enjoyable side of things and instead take whatever you are handed as is, then you are in for some miserable times. The true secret to life is how you choose to "show up" for it. Remember, it is still just a job; it is not life or death.

I left AT&T where I worked for 14 years to start my own business in 1993. I was the only income in a household with three small kids. Failure was not an option. I had made a high-risk decision with my career. I worked out of my home and my first desk was my son's Play-Doh Playskool desk. Seriously. It was orange and yellow and about two feet high. When I would type on it, I looked like Schroeder from the *Peanuts* cartoon, It was pretty funny when my son would want to play on his desk and I had to say, "Just a few more minutes, Daddy has to bang out this major proposal for GE." Believe me, it's tough to convince a small child on the importance of that versus making a clay dinosaur. It really is amazing when I think back on it. Trying to recruit great people was fun because not many people could place their faith in a guy who had an orange and yellow plastic desk. You have to be a pretty good visualizer (or maybe completely nuts) to see any potential there. Surprisingly though, two guys joined me right from the start and stayed with me for the long haul. I must give them major kudos for trusting enough in me to join up. They either trusted me or maybe they just liked my desk and wanted one too, but Chris Pratt and Loren Griswold came on board.

Chris and Loren were guys I trusted implicitly and I had known them before while working together at AT&T. I knew their work ethic and I knew they would be unshakably loyal to me. We worked together at AT&T for many years, and we always had fun. I convinced them to join my new company by telling them that we could do some great things, but most importantly we would have fun every day. Chris and Loren shared a passion for the training business and they were good at it. We had found something we loved doing and most of all we loved working together. Success came fast and furious. In truth, it almost came too fast. We had difficulty keeping up with the demand. I know, I know, that is a high-rent problem. I am not complaining at all, but I will tell you we accomplished some amazing things and the only way we kept our sanity was that we made work fun. The company grew to become a global leader in the field of sales training, and we had the most respected companies in the world seeking us out to work with them. In a very short time, the company became a world leader in the area of value creation and in high-level sales-skills training and our revenues soared. This meant I needed more great people like Chris and Loren.

Making Work Fun Works

At this time, we all still worked out of our homes. That was a great way to keep the people close to their families, and it also kept costs down. When I began interviewing people for new positions with the company, it was clear to me that the promise of giving them their lives back that corporate America had taken from them was a major attraction. We had all the people work from home, we emphasized the importance of a family-first approach to business, and we created a fun workplace. No one took themselves too seriously, and there was none of the typical corporate politics. When one person won, we all won. People supported and pulled for each other. It was a winning formula, and great people sought us out to work for us. My value proposition to my associates was to guarantee that not only will they have more fun, but they will be able to place their family first and focus on building their life worth. It was a bonehead-free environment. When you work for a large corporation as I did, you cannot control some of the people they hire. Now I had the control and if you were a bonehead, a taker or an energy "drainer," sorry, but this company was NOT for you. I don't care how excellent you think you are, I will give you an opportunity to be excellent "elsewhere."

Some people did slip through the cracks though. I did miss the signs early on when I hired a couple of people who cared only about themselves and ultimately proved themselves to be takers of the highest order. Once I caught on, "You're out!" I can't have that in my business nor can I have those people around me in my life. We did not treat our many customers as customers; they were our friends. We helped them when they needed it, and they always appreciated it and we were their first call when their businesses recovered. They also helped us when we needed it. Those are great relationships to have.

We actually fired some customers that we did not want to work with. A few customers acted in a way that demonstrated that they had no respect for people or their suppliers and tried to treat us badly so they could run to their own bosses internally and tell them how great they are because they stuck it to a little guy for a 5 percent discount. In many cases, that person's behavior was not indicative of the entire company's mentality, it was just an irrelevant person trying to make themselves relevant.

One time we were delivering a program in Europe where we used two instructors. It was not a requirement for the program; it was our choice as one instructor was more than adequate to deliver this program and we did not charge extra for the second instructor. We did it to reduce the pressure of having one person cover all the training and to provide the client another perspective in the classroom. At one point in the three-day program, the father of one of my facilitators passed away unexpectedly. His father had passed away in the

United States, so my first concern was that we had to get him back from Europe to his family as quickly as possible. We advised the customer of the situation and said we were pulling him out of the class and the second instructor would continue on with the program. No problem. The executives in Europe were fine with that decision and even helped us get him back to the States.

Later that evening I received a call from the procurement person from this company's HQ in California, requesting a discount on the price of this program since we now only had one instructor delivering it instead of two. Remember it was *our* decision to have two instructors as a favor to the company and we did *not* charge extra for this. That did not faze this procurement person; she wanted a 50 percent reduction in the program price, knowing that this person's father had just died. I went crazy. I said, "You want to try and capitalize on someone's personal tragedy so you can go to your boss and tell them how great you are because you got 50 percent off. Gee, maybe you could get a half-level promotion out of this, huh?" I could not hold my temper. Clearly I was speaking to an uncaring, selfish person who would stop at nothing just so she could "matter" to her higher-ups. I said I would *never* entertain her request and could not believe that someone could be so heartless for their own personal gain. I then called the senior vice president (her boss's boss's boss's boss) and told him what had happened and that we could no longer do business with his firm. No amount of money was worth dealing with people like that and we did not need his business that badly.

The senior vice president was appalled by the behavior we received and said he would handle it. I got a call back the next day and he apologized profusely, saying that procurement person would never trouble us again. I suspect she was either fired or appointed to open up their new Siberia office. Either way, she was done. He asked if I would please consider continuing our working relationship with his company. We did continue our relationship and they are clients to this day, 15 years later. I think he really respected that I took a stand for my people and would not compromise on my principles of only working with people we like and who are fun. In turn, I respected him for taking immediate action and demonstrating that this behavior would not be tolerated. I sure know that the rest of my people rallied and were in total support of my position, even if it meant costing them money. They did not care about the money. Right is right. That is why my company achieved such success and built one of the top client rosters in the world. I would put it up against any other company in our field. Not only were we good at what we did, but companies liked the way we did it, and that made us one of the top sales-training companies in the world. Even today I make it a practice to work with people whom I really want to work with. People who are fun, people whom I can learn and grow from. I absolutely love meeting new people. It is the best part of my job.

Having Fun Is Smart Business

In addition to being a public speaker, I am also a part-owner of several minor league baseball teams. The ownership group is famous for having fun. In fact, the business plan is only three words: "Fun Is Good." That's it. The results are astonishing. Some of the co-owners include such innovators as Mike Veeck, Bill Murray (yes, *that* Bill Murray), Al Fahden, Jimmy Buffet, Jimmy Fallon, Tom Whaley, and Marv Goldklang, to name just a few of the many great people who make it work.

Some of the promotions done at these games are groundbreaking and very funny. Go to a St. Paul Saints game in Minnesota sometime and you will see what I mean. There are hot tubs in the outfield, a pig that delivers baseballs to the umpire, a nun who gives massages in center field and barber chairs along the foul lines, just to cite a few of the in-stadium fun things offered. People love it. We have crazy promotions such as Inflatable Bat Night sponsored by Viagra and Lawyer Appreciation Night, where all lawyers were charged double for their tickets and an extra $1.00 for every inning they stayed (all proceeds went to the legal defense fund). We had Silent Night, where no one was allowed to make noise at the games. Instead they held up signs that say "Yeah" or "Boo" or "Beer Here." At our Brockton Rox baseball club in Brockton, Mass., we had Mime night, where we hired mimes to re-enact close plays for the fans on the dugout roof after we could no longer show them on the large centerfield electronic scoreboard because the league felt it would incite the crowd to potentially abuse the umpires. The first play the mimes tried to re-enact seemed to puzzle the Brockton Rox fans. They watched quizzically with their heads to the side much like "Nipper" the RCA Victor dog (for those of you old enough to remember Nipper). Then someone stood up and flung a hot dog at the mimes, hitting one square in the head. You could see the light bulbs illuminating in each fan's head. "This must be why those mimes are there. They are targets...cool!!" This prompted several thousand fans to throw their hot dogs at them as well. It was fun night—not for the mimes but it was fun for everyone else. Plus, we sold a ton of hot dogs.

Another promotion was for Enron. At the time, Enron was in the middle of being investigated for financial irregularities, destroying incriminating documents and "cooking the books." One of our ball clubs decided to pay tribute to Enron executives by hosting "Enron Appreciation Night." The tribute included having paper shredders at every entrance, and in the spirit of sound bookkeeping practices that Enron apparently was *not* practicing, we announced a different attendance figure at the end of each inning. For more on these promotions and the "Fun Is Good" approach to business, take a look at a book written by Mike Veeck called *Fun Is Good*. You'll learn just how much fun we have and the incredible effect it has on our employees, fans and the entire community. In the end, having fun is just smart business.

The Art of Savoring

A major contributor to fun and happiness is the art of "Savoring." This is the practice of slowing down so that you can take great pleasure in the simple things in life. Savoring is scientifically proven to increase your personal happiness. It is so important to savor moments as though they won't come again, because many of those moments really won't ever come again. It is funny because I can remember watching my grandfather get up very early in the morning just to enjoy the solitude of the morning and collect his thoughts. My father would often join him and that is when they had some of the most meaningful talks with each other without interruption. This was their time. My grandfather was an executive chef for some of the top resorts in the Adirondacks in Upstate New York. He would cook breakfast for my father and they would just sit and savor each other's company. I really found this tradition delightful, so much so that I did the very same thing with my father at every opportunity we had for 45 years until his passing. Breakfast was our time together. My mother just enjoyed watching father and son talk about anything in life and listening to wisdom being passed to each other (more wisdom from him to me than me to him, for sure). I would not trade those breakfast sessions for anything.

As people get older, they have a tendency to wake up earlier and earlier each day. I think they do this so they can savor as many moments in the day as they can. They are more aware that time is shortening for them so they want to catch every minute they can while they can. Here is a good way to remind yourself that we don't have much time on this Earth and that every day is to be enjoyed. Imagine that you are 45 years old and let's say that the average lifespan of a human being is 75 years. Well, there are 52 Saturdays in a year and you have 30 years left, according to our example. If you multiply 52 times 30 you get 1,560. That means you have about 1,560 Saturdays left in your life. To further emphasize the fleeting nature of life and why it is important to savor it, buy 1560 marbles and put them in a jar. Each Saturday that passes, simply remove one marble from the jar. As you watch the marble count in the jar dwindle, you can see how many Saturdays you have left. If the jar runs out of marbles and you are still enjoying life, then you are in the bonus round. Straight butter, baby!! It is a great way to be focused on not letting anything go to waste in terms of your time. Think about this when you get up on a Saturday and have to choose between cutting the grass or spending time creating a memory with your family or friends.

My parents were very good at the art of savoring. They took immense joy in the simple things. My father and mother used to love filling birdfeeders and watching the different types of birds come by and feed. These are the little things that bring a lot of pleasure. Today, I carry on this tradition by sitting and watching the birds eat from my own feeders. I will sit on my back deck every night and watch the trout jump in the lake. I love the smell of freshly cut grass, a real wood fire, the beauty of a full moon, crickets and frogs singing at night, the sound of kids laughing, the smell of fresh flowers, eating a hot tomato right out of the garden, the stillness of warm summer nights, the sounds of the whip-poor-wills in the forest and loons on the lake, clear nights filled with millions of stars, fall leaves at their peak, conversations with people who matter and lightly falling snow that glistens off the sun. The best things in life truly are free. If only people would take the time to enjoy them.

I wanted to share a poem that really hits the mark on the importance of savoring. Urban legend says that this poem was written by a young teenager with terminal cancer, but it was really written by David Weatherford.

SLOW DANCE

Have you ever watched kids on a merry-go-round,
or listened to rain slapping the ground?

Ever followed a butterfly's erratic flight,
or gazed at the sun fading into the night?

You better slow down, don't dance so fast,
time is short, the music won't last.

Do you run through each day on the fly,
when you ask "How are you?", do you hear the reply?

When the day is done, do you lie in your bed,
with the next hundred chores running through your head?

You better slow down, don't dance so fast,
time is short, the music won't last.

Ever told your child, we'll do it tomorrow,
and in your haste, not see his sorrow?

Ever lost touch, let a friendship die,

'cause you never had time to call and say hi?

You better slow down, don't dance so fast,
time is short, the music won't last.

When you run so fast to get somewhere,
you miss half the fun of getting there.

When you worry and hurry through your day,
it's like an unopened gift thrown away.

Life isn't a race, so take it slower,
hear the music before your song is over.

Take Risks, Savor Life and Leave a Legacy

I read a study that was done at a major university where more than 200 senior citizens (ages 80 and above) were asked to reflect on their lives and what would they do differently if they had an opportunity to do it again? Their answers centered around three distinct areas. The first thing they said they would do differently is that they would take more risks. Not because they were dissatisfied with their position in life, but because they remembered those times in their lives where they took risks and they had never felt more alive. It was exciting, a bit dangerous and they loved the fact that they had the guts to roll the dice. The other thought was that all those things they thought were risks in their 20s or 30s were not really big risks at all when they looked back on them now.

The second thing they said they would do differently was that they would "slow down." They would not be in a hurry to rush through life, especially when they were younger. They know how precious every day you have truly is and that is amplified when you are 80-plus.

Why couldn't they have understood this when they were in their 20s and 30s? We get bored with childhood, we rush to grow up, and then we long to become children again.

The third thing they said they would do is be more concerned about leaving a legacy. Not the kind of legacy that requires a statue of themselves in their villages or parks but a legacy that showed the world was somehow better because they made a difference. Remember the classic Jimmy Stewart movie *It's a Wonderful Life*? In this story, Jimmy Stewart's character George Bailey is under tremendous pressure and is overwhelmed with his responsibilities. The more he works, the less he seems to accomplish and the less people notice. He questions himself and feels that his life has had no meaning. On Christmas Eve, he tries to end his life and openly wishes that he had never been born. An angel grants him his wish and he is allowed to watch life progress all around him as though he was never born. The point is that after seeing how much of a difference he actually made in people's lives and just how good he really had it, George Bailey wants to go back to his old life. He did make a difference after all.

The theme of *It's a Wonderful Life* reflects what this study of senior citizens points out: leaving a legacy matters. What will they say at your funeral? In religious circles it is called testimony. I remember talking with a minister who had to give the final eulogy for his uncle. The minister was truly distraught. He said the only noteworthy thing he could say was that his uncle was a really good gardener. Can you imagine that? You live your whole life and the only thing people can say was that you were a good gardener? Are you kidding me? If ever there was a "Do Over" card, he probably should have played it a long time ago.

So there you are, wisdom for the ages from the aged. I always find it rewarding to spend time with people over the age of 70 and under the age of 6. I cannot tell you how much I learn from them. You can rationalize the wisdom from those who have lived more life than you, but how can kids teach you anything? I find kids to be painfully honest and that is refreshing. Let's face it, if a 6-year-old tells you that you are ugly, you are! Let me share with you the wisdom of children through the answers they gave when asked the question, "What is love?" Here is what they answered:

- *Love is when a girl puts on perfume and a boy puts on shaving cologne and they go out and smell each other.* Kari, age 5

- *Love is when you go out to eat and give somebody most of your French fries without making them give you any of theirs.* Crissy, age 6

- *Love is what makes you smile when you're tired.* Terri, age 4

- *Love is when my mommy makes coffee for my daddy and she takes a sip before giving it to him, to make sure the taste is OK.* Danny, age 7

- *Love is what's in the room with you at Christmas if you stop opening presents and listen.* Bobby, age 7

- *If you want to learn to love better, you should start with a friend who you hate.* Nikka, age 6

- *Love is like a little old woman and a little old man who are still friends even after they know each other so well.* Tommy, age 6

- *Love is when mommy gives daddy the best piece of chicken.* Elaine, age 5

- *Love is when your puppy licks your face even after you left him alone all day.* Maryann, age 4

- *Love is when mommy sees daddy on the toilet
  and doesn't think it's gross.* Marc, age 6

- *You really shouldn't say "I love you" unless you mean it. But if you
  mean it, you should say it a lot. People forget.*
  Jessica, age 8

The winner was a little boy, age 6:

- *When the child saw the neighbor cry, the little boy went over into the
  man's yard and climbed on top of the man's lap and just sat there.
  When the boy's mother asked him what he'd said to the neighbor, the
  little boy said, "Nothing, I just helped him cry."*

Out of the mouths of babes...

The Three Greatest Gifts

The final thought that I want to share about "Life Is Fun and Fun Is
Good" is about the three greatest gifts you can give your family. It fits
right into our discussion of the importance of slowing down and savoring
life. Believe it or not these gifts won't cost you a penny and they will last
forever. Your family will love you more than ever and these gifts are the
secret to creating life worth as a family. The three gifts? Simple.

1. Time
2. Memories
3. Tradition

Time is all your family wants from you. Time to know you, to enjoy
you, to laugh and time that they can count on and will never forget.
If you want to impress your family, give them your time. Time is the
vehicle to create memories.

Memories are the single most important thing we can give to our families. Memories keep families close when distance separates them. Memories have healed the sick, and they have made the loss of a loved one bearable. In the end, memories are your legacy. They are really all you have left.

Tradition is something you give your family that lives on long after you. Tradition is the stories that are told at gatherings, the family recipes grandma used to make, the family dinners, the movie nights, the vacation spots you went to year after year, and how you spend the holidays. Tradition is everything that your family will carry on after you leave them. That is how they carry the memory of you around with them forever and pass it on for generations.

Remember, these things don't cost you one cent. Focus on these and you will be a rock star and life worth will be yours.

CHAPTER SEVEN

Your "Last Lecture" to Your Family

"You have spent your whole life becoming the person you are today. Was it worth it?"

–Richard Bach

"Life is very much like a book. It has a definite beginning and a definite ending. But all the chapters in between are ours to write."

–Gary Kunath
(OK, so it's my second quote)

I think it is very important to surround yourself with people who care about you and who understand who you truly are and what you truly value. I mean a genuine, down-deep understanding. Sometimes we don't ever have those conversations that say, "This is who I really am and what matters most to me and this is what I know as a result of me roaming the planet for all these years."

We create wills for people to understand how we want our "stuff" divided up and who should get what. But we should take the opportunity to share with our loved ones who we really are as a person. I don't want my family guessing what I would have thought or how I would react or what really mattered to me. I want them to know these things from my own lips and preferably while I am alive so that we can grow together and strengthen our relationships.

There is a concept called an Ethical Will, which is a document designed to pass moral values from one generation to the next. I really like the idea behind it and I have modified it somewhat to shape into what I call your "Last Lecture" to your family. If you had to give one last lecture to your family, what would you tell them? What would you want them to know? I love this concept, which was made more widely known through the efforts of an incredible man named Randy Pausch, a professor at Carnegie Mellon University. I wrote this letter to my son two years prior to Professor Pausch's death and his famous speech to his class.

I wrote the following letter to my son Dan when he graduated from Miami University of Ohio in 2002. It was my gift to him along with some cash that I had been saving for him to use as a down payment on a home when the time came. I want to share it here in this book in its original form because I think people might find it beneficial and it might be something they want to do for their own families.

My Graduation Gift to You

Dan,

There are actually two gifts contained in this envelope. One is a gift that I have been fortunate enough to be able to provide to you for helping you start your life. I had been saving this for you for quite some time, always with the intention of giving it to you on your graduation day. This is for you to use only for the purpose of purchasing a residence when you are ready to do so. A father always wants to be able to give his children the best possible life they are capable of giving. This will help provide some security and it will be there for you when you are ready to settle into a home of your own.

I know that today is a day of mixed emotions. It is both a happy and proud time for you, as it should be. But it may also be a sad time as you are closing the chapter of a very significant time in your life. You have had a wonderful ride and it makes me tremendously more proud of the fact that I was blessed enough to have played a small role in your journey. I say a small role because as a parent you can only do so much. I would love to be able to take full credit for how you turned out, but I cannot do that. You are the rightful owner of all the credit. The many achievements you have had as a boy growing up, all the way through to today, where you stand as a man, are a direct result of the choices that you have made and of the effort surrounding those choices. While graduation can be a time of conflicting feelings, the honest truth is that this is merely another of life's many transitions. Every day from now on holds a tremendous opportunity to experience all that life has to offer and to help you grow into a man who can look back on his life and be proud of his choices and how he lived it.

I know that my earlier gift was special, but that is not the real gift that I want to give to you. At least it is my hope that you will value my true gift even more. Dan, what I want to share with you are some of the most important life lessons that I have learned through-out my life and pass them along to you. I want you to know what I view as important and what I have learned to value as essential in life. I have learned these things through my own mistakes, experi-ences, successes and observations, and through what I have learned from the many people who have touched my life in both positive and negative ways. It is my hope that these thoughts that I want to pass on to you will help guide and shape you as you continue your journey in life. I certainly have not been perfect and I sure don't consider myself that smart. But I have learned some things along the way and I want to give them to you now.

These are the things that I know to be true:

Lesson One: Life worth is far more important than net worth.

In fact, it is the only thing that matters at all. Life worth is the joy and contentment you get from life. It is the single most important reason to be given life at all. Many people place all of their efforts on creating net worth, thinking that life worth will automatically come as a byproduct of net worth. It does not work that way. Life worth does not come from net worth. There are so many people who have a tremendously high net worth and are miserable. But if you have a high life worth, it is impossible to be anything other than completely fulfilled. You do not have to have net worth to have life worth. Invest your time in the things that create value in your life. These are not material things like cars, boats, cash or the normal trappings most people mistake for life worth. I am talking about true life worth. Like making a difference in someone's life, unconditional love, staying true to your own principles and values, not rushing through life's experiences but savoring each moment as though it may never happen again, appreciating and valuing the beauty of family, creating memories for your children, giving with no expectation of getting anything in return, and having a strong spiritual foundation. These are only some of the things that contribute to life worth.

Lesson Two: Bad things happen to good people.

We can never predict the future events that are destined for us. But you can be sure that you will experience great things that will give you tremendous highs and you will unfortunately be faced with things that are not so nice. However, all of these things, the good and the bad, are meant to enable us to grow even stronger as a result. How you choose to allow these things to impact you is the real difference. When I watched my father die and had to say goodbye to him for the very last time, it was the most difficult thing I have ever had to do in my life. But even still, as hard as it was for me, it was the most powerful thing that has ever happened to me. I had no regrets. We had a strong relationship and there were no loose ends, there was nothing left unsaid. He knew I loved him and I knew he loved me because we showed each other that every day. He left knowing that and knowing that I would take care of his wife, my mother, which was the most important thing to him. He could be at peace. It also taught me that life is fleeting. It can end at any time, so you need to live life to its fullest. Try new things, meet new people, laugh a little more, tell the people you care about how you feel, be open to ideas and the thoughts of others, spend your time with people who matter and grow every chance you get. Whenever I encounter some type of adversity that I think is really big, I always ask myself, "If my life were to end tomorrow, would this really be important?" I have gained a great perspective from that experience that I carry with me today. Life is too short to be lived in misery.

Lesson Three: Create memories.

I truly believe that memories are one of the strongest and most sustaining life forces one can have. Memories have kept prisoners of war alive, they have healed the sick and sped up recovery times, they are a source of laughter and smiles, they keep loved ones close when they are miles apart, they are a source of motivation, of hope, of gratification and of comfort in troubled times. But the most important thing about memories is that they represent your life's legacy. When people remember you, what will you want them to remember about you? Ultimately, memories will be the only thing that you will have at the end. It won't be money or any type of material thing, it will be what you think about when you look back at your life. Memories are the single most important thing for anyone and you should focus your life around creating memories for yourself and for your children. If you create great memories you will always have a place to go when times are tough. The true test is when you and your kids can say, "Remember when?" and everyone smiles. Make this a priority in your life.

Lesson Four: Grow a little from everyone you meet.

Dan, I want to share two thoughts here with you. The first is that I believe everyone has a unique gift within them that makes them special. It is very important you look for that gift and respect it. No one is perfect and we all have our flaws, but judge people on their gifts and look at the entire person before you make a decision about them. If you prejudge or discount people because you see something about them that you do not agree with or like, don't be quick to disregard them. If you do, you may be missing a wonderful opportunity to grow. You will find that of the people who come into your life, some will have much more good than bad in them, some will have equal amounts of good and bad and, frankly, some will be tremendous cement heads. My point is simply that you can grow from every one of these people. I have learned as much from the boneheads as I have from the truly great ones. Even if the lessons are that I never want to be like them because I felt the pain of what they are and how they act. This ability to learn from everyone is tremendously valuable.

You have to look for the life lessons in each person that you meet and listen carefully for their gifts, as they all will represent an opportunity to make you a better person. The second thought is that when I look at who I am, many people might say "Oh, That's Gary

Kunath." That is true, I am Gary Kunath. But how I became who I am is a culmination of the many people whom I have met over my life who have influenced me in both positive and negative ways. I was able to learn from everyone I met and all of them shaped the type of person that I am today through what I experienced and what I learned. I do not want you to miss out on this opportunity.

Lesson Five: Don't major in the minors.

Since we all have such limited time here on Earth, it is important to find those things that are truly important to you and really matter and then spend your time there. Don't spend your time in areas that don't matter. Too many people really focus on stuff that ultimately means nothing. Work can be one of those things that consume you. I know from experience on that one. It will never happen to me again. Someone told me once with regard to our focus on selling to our customers, "How come we spend so much time trying to impress people that we don't even know?" I thought about that a lot, and he was right. If you were only given $5 and it had to last you two weeks, how would you spend it? More than likely, you would spend it on only the most important things. That is the same as life. You only have a small amount of time and you need to ask yourself, how will you spend it?

Lesson Six: Build a strong faith.

This is truly the foundation of life worth. You will encounter things in life that will require that you have a strong faith. You have to know that there is a higher power and faith is the one thing that will keep you going even when you think you cannot go any farther. I have seen it and experienced it for myself. When your high school friend was killed in that car accident, faith was the only thing that pulled his family through. When terminal illness visits a family, faith is the only thing that pulls them through it. When unexpected tragedy hits, it is your faith that will be your guiding force. Make building your spiritual strength a priority. You will need this as you go through life, and be sure to give this gift to your children.

Lesson Seven: Take immense pleasure in the simple things.

When I think back to when you were a child, the most fun and memorable things did not cost a cent. You took immense joy in simply throwing stones in the water to watch the splash, feeding the chipmunks at camp, catching a fish, listening to the bullfrogs under a full moon, swimming in the lake, driving a car solo for the first time, watching butterflies land near you, catching lightning bugs, getting your first "A" in school, bringing your new best friend home for the first time, the first sleepover, and running around our old neighborhood banging old pots and pans at midnight on New Year's Eve. All of these things and many more were just simple things. But they were more than that because they turned into great memories and they had no dependency on income levels. They were free and so are all the best things in life. Take the time to enjoy them.

Lesson Eight: Care about others.

This is a huge thing. Every action that you take affects other people. What you say, how you say it, what you do, how you do it, the time you spend, where you spend it...everything will have an impact on others. You need to be aware of the effect of your actions and factor it into all of your decisions. For example, you told me that you were not going to attend the smaller of the two graduation ceremonies because you felt it would be boring and a waste of time. You wanted to spend that time with friends instead. As I write this, I do not know the final decision you will have made on this. But I do know this fact: You were only thinking of yourself. You need to understand that this is not just your graduation, it is our graduation too. All of the hard work, sacrifices, hopes and dreams that we have all had for you will be represented in this weekend. We are immensely proud of you and of your achievement, and we view this as the culmination of our life's work to give you every possible opportunity to have an even better start than we had. I cannot say that attending the smaller graduation on Saturday will or won't be the right thing to do. Maybe it will be boring as you suggested, maybe Sunday's graduation ceremony is all that is needed. I don't know. But I do know that you did not think about your decision from our perspective at all or about what this weekend means to us. You only looked at it from your perspective. That attitude will not serve you well in life. Remember, everything you do will impact others in some way, so you must always think through that fact when you consider the options and ask, how will this impact the people I care about and who care about me? Then ask yourself, is this really the best decision and am I doing the right thing or my thing?

Lesson Nine: Strengthen your relationships with your brothers.

They love you more than you know and they look up to you as a hero. They always have. Just the fact that they always talk about you and ask for your old jersey number when they play sports should tell you this. All they want in return is to see you show them that they matter to you. You are very lucky to have two tremendous brothers who are very different from each other and from you, but both have unique gifts and are truly the finest people that I know. They will need your guidance, your demonstrated love, your support, your closeness and most of all they need to have some of your time. I need to know that if something ever happens to me where I cannot watch out for them that you will be there for them in my place. Take time out to call them on the phone, talk to them, take them to lunch, have them visit you, take an interest in things that are important to them even if they are not important to you, learn about them and most of all show them that they matter to you. It won't take much, but the results will astonish you.

Lesson Ten: Have fun.

If it is not fun, don't do it. You might think that there will be some things that are not fun that you will have to do anyway. Like going to a funeral, for example. That's true, funerals are not fun at all, especially if it's your funeral. Here is my outlook: If you truly focus on having fun in the many other aspects of your life, then when you have to do something that is not so fun, the good times will sustain you and see you through it. My other thought here is that there are many things that we do where there are tremendous opportunities to have fun, but because we don't think like that, we miss out. For example, a job can be fun or it can be draining. Which one really depends on your outlook and how you choose to play it. Being transferred to a new city could be devastating for some people because it means being uprooted. But you can make that same move a terrifically exciting opportunity to meet new people, experience new things and add some adventure and spice to your life. It is all about looking forward and not backward, and it is about your mindset and how you choose to let things affect you. It costs nothing to smile, to laugh, to learn from new people, to watch sunsets and sunrises, and to focus on the positive and let go of the negative. In other words, having fun is within your control and the effect on those around you is contagious.

Well I am all out of life lessons. (I figure ten is a pretty good number anyway.) The last thing I want to tell you is that life is really much like the game of golf. You will have shots that will excite and amaze you, shots where you will wonder how you did that. You will also have shots that might make you angry, and if you string several of those bad shots together you may even want to quit the game. Many people do quit the game. The game of life, that is. To me, that is a travesty. I have had my share of bad shots, but to quit is just not the right thing to do. It is just not in my mentality to even think about quitting. Besides, there are too many people who are depending on me. When I quit on myself, I also am quitting on them. I can't do that. I can't quit. The reason is that in golf, like life itself, your next shot may be your best ever. You can have a poor front nine, but make some changes and have the best back nine of your whole career. That is exactly what life is all about. I believe that no matter what you do in life or the mistakes that you might make, you can always redeem yourself with your next opportunity. Maybe you just change your grip, or maybe alter your swing slightly. Maybe it is a more major problem like having to buy a new set of clubs. No matter what it is, it's always salvageable. You can always get better, learn from your mistakes and persevere, and have the best back nine of your life. I have always been the type of person who looks forward and if I look backward at all, it is to see briefly where I have been and to use that experience to make me better tomorrow.

Dan, I tried to give to you some of my views and beliefs on what I have learned over the course of my life. I am sure that I will continue to learn and will be able to add to this list someday. For now though, I think this is a good recipe for success and for having a high life worth. I am so proud of you and what you have done. I always have been proud of you and always will be. All my life I have worked hard to give you, Dave and Tom the best life I could give you. While I have had my share of successes, when I look back on my 46 years on this earth, there is nothing—and I mean nothing—that compares to having been blessed with such a terrific set of sons. That is my best accomplishment of all! I cannot tell you how much I love each of you. I would give my life for each of you without a second's hesitation. My goal is to grow closer to each of you, not farther away, to know you more, not less, and to love you more each day that passes and to show it. When that day comes when it is finally my time to pass, I want you to feel as comfortable about our relationship as I did when my father passed. I want us to have absolutely no regrets. I want to leave knowing that we had a strong relationship and there were no loose ends or words left unsaid, me knowing that you loved me and you knowing that I loved you because we showed each other that every day. Then I will know that my life had meaning and that I was able to do a few things right.

Start living your life lessons right now by savoring your achievements and once again, congratulations! You earned this; now enjoy it!

All My Love,

Dad

CHAPTER EIGHT

Random Thoughts from a Not So Random Guy

"Death is not the greatest loss in life. The greatest
loss is what dies inside us while we live."

—Norman Cousins

"The best things in life are not things."

–Art Buchwald

T his is my time to do some organized rambling about things I truly believe in or things that bug me. So sit back and try to keep up.

Let's Teach Our Kids More Life Skills in School

We really need to teach our kids the "life skills" that they need to succeed in any endeavor they choose. Some of the things kids have to learn in school are outdated and irrelevant. For example, is there any job on the planet that requires you to know how to diagram a sentence? Why do we teach that? I have never been asked to find the dangling participle of anything in my life, and I am 53 years old. My guess is that I probably won't get asked for the rest of my life. I have seen that some of the books I was required to read 35 years ago are still some of the same books we require of our kids today. I get it; the *Moby Dicks*, the *Billy Buds*, the *Catcher in the Ryes*, etc. are considered classics, but haven't any great books been written in the last 40 years? Books that may spark more interest, simply because of their currency? We have to teach our kids math to build their analytical skills, and history, science and all of that is important to give them a good foundation from which to build. The problem is that these subjects when taught "as is" with no context leave students bored. They lose interest because too often they have no idea *why* they need these courses or what skills they will acquire from them. We need to do more than just teach material to children. We need to give them the context of that material, that is, what they're learning and why it will help them later in life. There are some great teachers who help their students understand how these subjects will enable them to think more deeply or to be able to understand life outside the classroom. Showing kids the "why" behind the "what" is critical.

Our kids need to be exposed to more life skills in the classroom and at an earlier age. What are life skills? Skills like leadership, interpersonal communication, innovation and creative thinking, conflict resolution, personal resiliency, negotiation, public speaking, the art of persuasiveness, balancing a checkbook, how to get a loan, and how to pay your bills. Learning a language should be mandatory from an early age, not just two years in high school, but let's start them learning a language in elementary school, when it's easiest for them to pick it up. Learning a second or even a third language is a tremendous advantage to our ability to compete globally and for our kids to enhance their own marketability in the job market. If two kids are vying for a job with an international company, the one who speaks multiple languages fluently has a definite advantage.

We need to teach our kids these skills and not wait for them to go to college to acquire them. Of course you will have to position the various programs and construct the content in an age-appropriate way, but waiting until college to maybe get exposed to these life skills is way too late. Even in college many of these skills are not addressed. Let's make life skills a one- or two-credit course, at the very least in ALL curriculums regardless of your degree track. We also need to expose the kids to some of the "Life Worth" ideas I've talked about in this book. What are the secrets to happiness? Why does life worth matter? The importance of savoring, showing gratitude, expressing acts of kindness, and learning to forgive are all skills that drive and determine your personal happiness. College teaches skills that help students make a living, but it is also an excellent place for them to be taught how to make a life.

Broaden Understanding and Appreciation of Other Cultures by Experiencing Them

Everyone should have the benefit of an international experience. Whether it is a job, an internship, a study-abroad program, personal travel or a family vacation, the experience and growth international travel affords is priceless. I travel all over the world and actually live in Italy part of the year. I have come to understand that people everywhere are very similar. People in China like to laugh as much as people in Italy; people in Brazil love great food just like people in Germany; people in Canada love their sports just like people in Spain. In Italy, for example, they value their family time. In fact, most businesses shut down in the afternoon so that people can have lunch (their most important meal) with their families.

A major reason we see a lot of angst between cultures is that we have a serious lack of understanding and knowledge about other cultures. If you don't understand another culture, you can't appreciate the reasons behind why they do what they do or why they feel how they feel. Even in the United States we have no true appreciation for another person's journey. Jackie Robinson, the first black professional baseball player, had it written in his contract that he could not react if fans spit on him. How could you relate to that? I have a good friend who is black and he is very successful, but even so he told me that when he purchases items in stores he is always asked for multiple forms of identification beyond his Platinum Amex card while the three white people in front of him are not ever asked. I never knew that and when he told me, I completely understood why that made him mad. I would be mad too. In contrast, I mentioned to him that I was denied a promotion for a job opening because I was a white male and the company needed a minority for their HR numbers, even though I was well qualified. I was told this directly, off the record, by the hiring executive. I was not even given a chance, I was told not to even apply. It was also not the first time it happened to me either. He never knew that and he understood how that could make me mad. We surely opened each other's eyes that day. I am not trying to be controversial here, I am simply saying that when we expose ourselves to different cultures and experiences we develop more insight and, I believe, more understanding and tolerance. It also removes the misperceptions we have due to our ignorance. Every one of us is ignorant; we're all just ignorant about different things.

Wearing Pajamas to the Airport

When I see kids wearing PJs at the airport, nothing screams, "Hey look at me, I am too lazy to get up early, I only care about myself, I value sleep more than pride in how I look!" more than that. I look at their parents and it tells me that they have decided it was not worth fighting the fight and they will just let their children show up however they want as long as they don't miss their flight. They are feeding the monster. And you know what happens when you do that: the monster gets bigger.

Wearing Pants Below Your Butt

I shake my head when I see this, especially when matched with wearing a hat sideways with the hologram stickers and price tags still on the hat. Yikes, are you kidding me? Do you have a mirror in your house? Whenever I see someone wearing their pants this low, I think, "This is an individual who has no sense of self." They are followers. Not only do you look goofy, but it dramatically reduces your ability to get a job. I know it sounds unfair, but people do judge you on how you act and how you dress. This style may be acceptable to your friends but I can tell you it definitely sends the wrong message to everyone else. Please consider being yourself and dress in a way that will carry you beyond the moment, don't be a follower, and parents, please share with your kids that even though it may be a "phase" they are going through, it does not serve them well. Distinction, uniqueness, style and class will take you far in life. Pull up your pants, don't show us your underwear and walk tall, it really does matter.

Create a Master Dream List

Aim at nothing and you will hit it every time. It is important to have life goals, those things you want to accomplish in your life before your time is up. I have a master dream list. I have things on it like learn a language, catch a marlin, climb Mount Kilimanjaro, write a book (check this one off the list), etc. I may not get to do them all, but I know that I will get to none of them if I don't focus on them.

Watch the movie *The Bucket List*. It's a great movie and it explains better than I can why you need a master dream list.

The Two Greatest Dissatisfactions in Life

I had the opportunity to co-present at a business event with Tom Morris, who at the time was a philosophy professor at Notre Dame University. Professor Morris is an insightful speaker and his approach was to take the thoughts from the greatest thinkers of all time—the great philosophers—and relate them to modern day. I credit the following points to him. Professor Morris says there are two major dissatisfactions in life: the Dissatisfaction of Acquisition and the Dissatisfaction of Aspiration. One is deadly and the other is very healthy for you.

Dissatisfaction of Acquisition is all about trying to replace gaps in your life with things. What you find is that no matter how many things you acquire, the gaps in your life not only don't close but they become larger. Hip-hop impresario Russell Simmons wrote in his book on leadership *Do You!* that when he first became successful and the money started rolling in, he went out and bought a Bentley car, which runs about $280,000. He was so excited and when he got it home, he drove it around his neighborhood about 10 times. Then he parked it and got out and realized that he did not feel any different after purchasing and driving the car than when he didn't own it. What he learned was that while he thought this expensive car would make him happy and feel differently about himself, none of that happened. He was no better off after he got the car than before he got it, except that he was out $280K. He said he will never make that mistake again.

That is why you see many people with money who have their lives derailed. You might say, how could they do that? Their life is perfect.

They have tons of money. What you don't realize is that the problem is "Access and Excess." These folks can buy anything they want and as much as they want. When we save up enough money to go to Disney World and we ride Space Mountain, it is unbelievable. We ride it once or maybe twice depending on the waiting line and it is awesome. If you ride Space Mountain 100 times in a row, the feeling gets numbed. It is not so cool and worse yet it becomes boring. So you look for the next big thing to excite you. Those that can afford it keep going higher and higher trying to keep exciting themselves until finally they run out of options. That is when the trouble starts. Things can never fill gaps in your life. This is a deadly assumption.

Dissatisfaction of Aspiration has to do with being dissatisfied with your own aspirations and achievement of them. This is a good thing. You aspire to have more knowledge, more experiences, and more memories. How much is too much? The answer is that the pursuit of these things only makes you better and that is all good.

Songs That Make You Think Deeply About Life and Have a Great Message

What a Wonderful World	Louis Armstrong
I Believe I Can Fly	R Kelly
Remember When	Alan Jackson
My Next 30 Years	Tim McGraw
But For the Grace of God	Keith Urban
The Prayer	Celine Dion and Andrea Bocelli
Good Stuff	Kenny Chesney

The River	Garth Brooks
In My Daughters' Eyes	Martina McBride
Cats in the Cradle	Harry Chapin
You Raise Me Up	Josh Groban
Live Like You Were Dying	Tim McGraw
Next Thing on My List	Toby Keith
Sailing	Rod Stewart
My Wish	Rascal Flatts

The Importance of Saying "Thank You"

This may seem trivial, but trust me it's not. There are many ways to express your gratitude, and it is critical that you make this a life practice. People will always remember a phone call, public acknowledgement or a handwritten note of thanks. I am a huge fan of handwritten thank-you notes. The most important and easiest thing you can do to make people feel really good and to distinguish yourself from all others is to get into the practice of sending thank-you cards. I am not talking about just for wedding gifts; whenever someone does something nice for you that you appreciate, send them a handwritten thank-you note.

A handwritten note shows that you took time out of your day to express your gratitude. Do yourself a favor, buy a box of thank-you cards and keep them with you to use often. In the past, when I have received them I can tell you I truly value them and they stick out in my memory, as do the people who have sent them to me. I have a box of them that I have saved over the years and I reread them occasionally just because they make me feel good. You will never find an easier or more significant way to make someone feel terrific and remember you than this. It only takes the cost of a stamp and about six minutes of time for a good deed that will be remembered for a very long time.

Make It a Point to Eat Dinner as a Family

We don't do this enough. It doesn't count when the kids are home for dinner and they take their plates in their rooms and text their friends or play video games. I mean you eat meals at the table and *talk* to each other. I have a friend, Neil Kimball, who actually created a concept called Family Table Time. He actually left a great job in corporate America to start his own company dedicated to bringing families closer together through having them eat more dinners together. It is a huge effort that literally is changing peoples' lives and reconnecting families. One of the things he provides is a kit that contains a tablecloth families can use that facilitates dinner table conversation and teaches important skills for ongoing family communication. It has questions to start conversation, places to write down key events and important milestones and everyone gets to write them all down ON the tablecloth. What a great idea! Be sure to check it out on www.thekimballcompanies.com. At the year's end, you have a tapestry of the year and of all the discussions and happenings from that year. If you don't eat meals as a family, make this an immutable in your household. No exceptions. Do it at least three days a week and for sure on the weekends.

Importance of Being a Good Communicator

I cannot stress this point enough. It is absolutely critical for people to have good communication skills. It is very telling when you listen to people who have a poor command of vocabulary and are unable to express themselves in a way that others can understand. For example, when I hear people use the word "irregardless," I quiver. Why? Because no such word exists. When people use it, it sends unflattering signals to others about them. Don't use it. I remember attending an executive-training class where the instructor was introducing himself and said he was a part-time college professor, in an effort to establish his credibility with the group of executives. The very next sentence he used the word "irregardless" and I saw one of the executives turn to the person next to him and whisper, "Obviously he is not an English professor." It just stuck with me and I know that this instructor never truly recovered in the mind of that exec, no matter what he said from that point forward. Little things like that count. There was a study done with 300 senior executives where the executives were asked to identify the single most important skill they felt was critical to their professional success. Hands down, the answer was communication skills. Strengthen your vocabulary, improve your ability to speak in public and practice good listening skills. It amazes me how few people actually listen. The main reason relationships fail is an inability to communicate and listen to each other. Just turn on any radio talk show where the host interacts with callers and count how many times they interrupt each other. It is staggering. Communication skills will carry you far in life, maybe even to the presidency.

Don't Give Your Kids Things, Make Them Earn It

Giving kids things they want makes them weak while making them earn what they want makes them strong. Parents at times feel guilty for not spending more time with their kids. It may be due to work, extensive travel or other outside commitments. They also fall prey to social and peer pressures placed on their kids by what other parents do and what other kids have, so the parents give their kids things to compensate. Don't buy into this approach. I know this from experience. If there was one thing I would do differently, it would be to make my kids earn their way more than I had them do. Have your kids earn their way to acquire what they want. I shoveled snow all around my neighborhood when I was 10 years old for $2 to $4 a driveway. And there sure were some really long driveways on my block. I graduated into having my own paper route where I delivered newspapers to everyone at their homes and collected the cash weekly from each person. Then I worked at Burger King and on my "off" days sold sodas at the Utica Memorial Auditorium at hockey games to pay my way through college. I bought my own car when I was young—it had well over 100,000 miles on it but it was all mine. I wouldn't trade that for anything In W. Randall Jones' book *The Richest Men in Town*, the most common denominator that all of the wealthiest people in the US pointed to as a key factor in their success was that they all worked when they were kids. They earned what they got and it was a life lesson that served them well to this day. Make this a rule and stick to your guns. Your kids will love you for it 10 years from now.

Should I or Shouldn't I Do the Right Thing?

I know I mentioned it earlier in this book but I feel strongly about this so I am going to add some additional thoughts on this topic. When my mother was in the hospital on the weekend that she died, I remember coming out of her room and the nurses station was in the center of the corridor with all of the rooms surrounding it in a full circle. What I remember was overhearing a conversation in the room next to my mothers. The rooms were open and I could not help but hear what was going on in this family conversation. They were there because their father was dying and he was on life support. They had made the decision to remove him from life support but were waiting because one of the sons couldn't come immediately because he had an important business meeting that he couldn't miss. There seemed to be great angst over this sons' decision to put his meeting over the passing of his Dad. I was stunned and to this day I wonder where that train went off the tracks? How did his relationship with his Dad and family get to a point where he felt that this business meeting took priority? How did he rationalize it in his head? What things did he convince himself of that in his mind made it OK to put business before the death of his father? I also wonder if his father knew that this was going on? Sure maybe he was physically not able to deduce what was happening but I always wonder if spiritually he knew. Strange and powerful things are at play in these types of situations. Things we cannot comprehend. If you read anything about near death experiences or peoples' accounts of what happens when a loved one passes, you cannot help but think that there are greater forces that we can ever understand at work. To this day, I wonder how will this son live with that decision? Will there ever come a time in his life when he will regret that move? How will he ever reconcile it in his head or with his family?   My simple thinking here is that there will come a day when he realizes that he should have been there. Maybe it will happen later in life or maybe even it will happen to him when one of his kids makes the same decision about him. My point here is that if he did not want to be there for his father for whatever reason, he should have been there for himself.

I have a friend that had an estranged relationship with his dad. They rarely spoke and when they did it was not a very good outcome. When his dad was terminally ill and he had to decide if he should go or not, he came to me to talk about it. The relationship was distant to say the least and there were a lot of unresolved issues between them. When he shared his situation with me, I could see he was torn apart by not knowing what to do. I simply told him that if there was ever a chance to repair some of the damage done over the years, it would never happen if he did not go see his dad. Most importantly though I told him that maybe he would never resolve any issues with his dad. One thing for sure was that he would always wonder about what might have been if he could have gone and didn't. I told him that it was more important to go for himself. He needed to do the right thing for himself or he would always hold himself accountable in some way for not going. This was a burden he did not need to place on himself. It was bad enough to know that he missed most of his life with his dad, but that was not solely his choice. He had tried to reconcile with his dad for years but his dad was either unwilling or didn't know how. But this situation was purely his to call, no one else. He had to go for himself. Even if there was no improvement in the relationship, he could sleep at night knowing that he did the right thing in the end by being there. As it turned out he went and it was the right call. He and his father connected and there was peace on both sides when he passed. Not going would have haunted him and this was a burden he would have to live with forever. He did the right thing for himself and it turned out to be the right thing for them both.

So when you are faced with decisions like this, I advise you to always do the right thing. It is not always the easiest thing to do and that's why so few people do It. Everyone knows what the right thing to do is even if they say they don't, they do. Follow your instincts and always think about how you will feel down the road about yourself if you choose to not do what is right. Then do it for yourself because you do not want to second guess yourself later in life. Do it for YOU.

Final Thoughts

I wrote this book in an attempt to share with people my life journey and how I came to learn what truly matters in life. It's the story of how I reshaped my thinking and my priorities to gain the most joy and contentment from my life. I want to tell people how easy it is to get caught up in the spin cycle of life and get off track as to what it is really all about. I know this because it happened to me. You can easily miss weeks, months, possibly years, and some miss life entirely by focusing on the wrong stuff. I almost did that myself. I have come full circle, from chasing the acquisition of money, houses and goofy things that once acquired, offer a very fleeting satisfaction. Now I find the greatest joy and contentment in taking my grandkids for a walk in the snow while I point out different birds and squirrels to them. The things that used to consume me and get in the way, I have dismissed and replaced with things I believe truly contribute to having a full and great life. As a friend once said to me, "You only go this way once, and when you're dead ,it's for a long time." I try to live life to its fullest every day. I take joy in meeting new people, laughing a lot, taking long walks, savoring simple moments, taking risks and trying new things, being grateful and expressing it sincerely, helping others, believing in something bigger than me and just simply being good and doing good.

I think we've come back to where we've started. You could have all the net worth in the world and if you can't spend time with the people you love and you are not happy, then you don't have anything of real value. I hope you've found the ideas in this book helpful and that you are able to put them to use in your life. Have fun, savor the good times and remember it's not about cash, it's about contentment. As singer/songwriter Zac Brown said in his hit song *Chicken Fried*, "There's no dollar sign on peace of mind, this I've come to know." So enjoy life with all of your might as that is all that truly matters. And the next time someone anonymously buys me dinner, I'll think that maybe it was you.

About the Author

Gary Kunath is the founder of The Summit Group, a recognized thought leader that provides high-end sales training and consulting to Fortune 500 companies.

He created a best practice around value creation which was awarded "Innovative Practice of the Year" by 3M worldwide. Clients include: Cisco Systems, General Mills, Hilton, AT&T, P & G, Xerox, Intel, HP, SC Johnson, Motorola, Lockheed, Marriott, Delta Air Lines, IBM, Fidelity, Textron, Tetra Pak, USPS, Microsoft and Ritz Carlton to name a few.

Gary serves on the Board of Trustees for Utica College. He was named "Businessman of the Year" and was formally recognized for this achievement at a dinner hosted by the President of the United States.

Gary is part owner of several professional minor league baseball teams. He is an equity partner in Bite Tech, makers of Under Armour's High Performance Mouth Wear, worn by over 400 professional athletes and sold in all major sporting goods stores across North America.

He holds an MS degree in Organizational Development from the State University of New York at Binghamton, and a BS degree in Business Administration/Marketing from Utica College of Syracuse University. He is also an August 1990 graduate of Duke University's Executive Development Program.

Gary is a highly sought after speaker and lecturer. His fun and energetic style makes him one of the most successful and in demand speakers on the circuit today. His topics include sales, value creation, leadership, elevating employee performance and of course; how to get the most joy and contentment from your life.

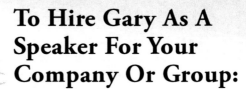

To Hire Gary As A Speaker For Your Company Or Group:

Call: (770)-594-2657

E-mail: **gmkunath@gmail.com**

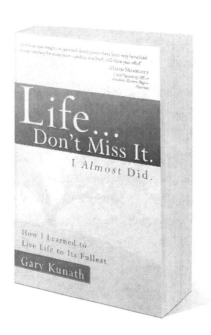

How can you use this book?

MOTIVATE

EDUCATE

THANK

INSPIRE

PROMOTE

CONNECT

Why have a custom version of *Life...Don't Miss It?*

- Build personal bonds with customers, prospects, employees, donors, and key constituencies

- Develop a long-lasting reminder of your event, milestone, or celebration

- Provide a keepsake that inspires change in behavior and change in lives

- Deliver the ultimate "thank you" gift that remains on coffee tables and bookshelves

- Generate the "wow" factor

Books are thoughtful gifts that provide a genuine sentiment that other promotional items cannot express. They promote employee discussions and interaction, reinforce an event's meaning or location, and they make a lasting impression. Use your book to say "Thank You" and show people that you care.

CPSIA information can be obtained at www.ICGtesting.com
Printed in the USA
LVOW131758300812

296719LV00018B/25/P